IF YOU KNEW YOU COULD
CHANGE YOUR LIFE
IN ONE WEEKEND
AND CLEAR OUT THE COBWEBS
OF YOUR PAST WITH
COLOR
AND A BRUSH,
WOULD YOU DO IT?

―――――

MOLL ANDERSON

CHANGE YOUR
HOME
CHANGE YOUR
LIFE™

WITH
COLOR

WHAT'S YOUR
COLOR STORY?

MOLL ANDERSON

CHANGE YOUR HOME CHANGE YOUR LIFE™

WITH COLOR

MOLL ANDERSON

In Loving Memory...

*Kitty Moon Emery was first and foremost the quintessential lady. She never uttered an inappropriate word, never raised her voice, and always supported what she believed in. If you were lucky enough to be in her life, then you were and are truly blessed. Kitty was an icon in the city she loved the most, Nashville, Tennessee. She worked tirelessly to help make Nashville a great place. Her list of accomplishments is remarkable and the ones you don't often hear about are forever amazing and life-changing. Kitty was my dearest girlfriend and my mentor. She believed in me when I could barely muster the strength alone. She took the time to read my chicken scratch on a legal-sized yellow pad (the entire yellow pad, I might add) and told me that I really did have something to say. She told me I could write and she continued to encourage me throughout the journey of my career—even from her last words at her "Celebration of Life". Kitty had written a letter for the minister to read at her service with messages to her loved ones. It was an incredible gift to all of us. She even managed to pitch this book from heaven! Kitty loved me with her incredibly huge heart that I have never seen in another human being. My heart is now heavy but so grateful that she is no longer suffering from the pancreatic cancer that took her life. It may have taken her body, but, even until her last breath, her beauty, class, strength and grace were all we could see. I am so thankful for God giving me this Angel here on earth and I have no doubt she will continue to watch over those she loved from her very special place in heaven. **I love you Kitty Sue!***

First published in the United States of America in 2017 by Post Hill Press, Franklin, Tennessee

Printed in Italy
10 9 8 7 6 5 4 3

EAN: 978-1-937268-05-3

Cover & Interior Design: Sheri Ferguson Swisher, Ferguson Design Studio,
    and Moll Anderson, Moll Anderson Productions
Publisher/Managing Editor: Cindy Games, Moll Anderson Productions
Copyeditor: Lisa Grimenstein, Billie Brownell
Interior Design & Photo Styling: Moll Anderson, Moll Anderson Productions
Photo Styling & Creative Coordinator: Ashley Cate, Moll Anderson Productions

www.mollanderson.com

DEDICATION

This book is dedicated to my son, Michael, and his wife, Aphrodite, who personify everything I write about in my books. They truly live a full sensory life. Their marriage is a true partnership and I could not be more proud of the life they are building together. Even their wedding was a reflection of the special couple they are, as they planned it together in such a way that allowed everyone a glimpse into their relationship and the love they share. As a life stylist and proud mom, I was so impressed by their attention to detail and my son's passion as a groom. They have created a warm and inviting home together, entertaining guests during lively Super Bowl celebrations, comical ugly Christmas sweater parties, and beautiful, thoughtful dinner parties and gatherings. Their love of travel and adventure has placed them at so many important events in the lives of those who are dear to them.

And just when things couldn't get more exciting, on August 10, 2016, they welcomed my granddaughter, Adrianna Melina, into the world. What an amazing feeling to see my child holding his child for the first time. Once again, I've watched as Aphie and Mike participate in a beautiful dance of partnership, this time as parents, effortlessly slipping into the roles of Mommy and Daddy.

So really, this book is dedicated to all three of them: Michael, Aphrodite, and Adrianna.

This very new and exciting beginning is what life is all about. They have changed their home by bringing a new and special life into it, transforming their lives for the better, forever. And what a thrill it will be to watch Adrianna's Color Story unfold as she grows up!

Love, Mom aka Gigi

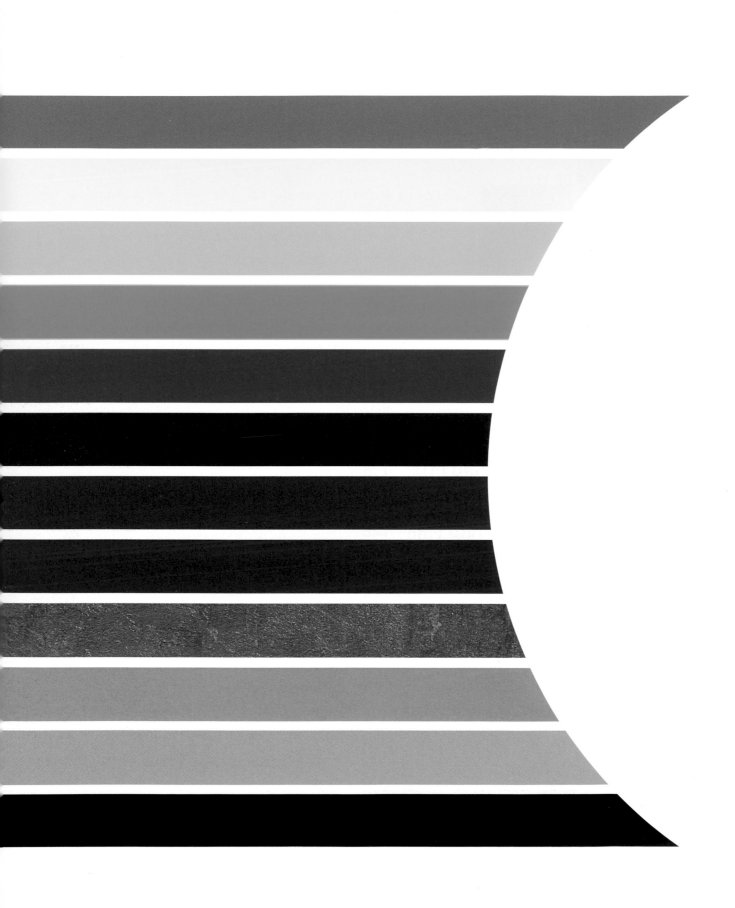

CONTENTS

FOREWORD

It's a summer afternoon at my local flower shop on the Pacific Coast Highway in Malibu, and I'm shooting a vlog with my BFF. I'm dressed in a grape Prada dress, Moll is wearing a purple bohemian silk top and tattered boyfriend jeans, and we are surrounded by a sea of mauve gardenias while arranging fuchsia orchids. We're in a purple haze, and Moll is tripping out on a full-blown color high, painting the background of our next shot like an enchanted artist. We lounge on a lavender velvet sofa and I see her size up its potential. "If I had a place for this beauty, I would buy it right now," she announces, declaring her full adoration for this weirdly shaped, obnoxiously lavender behemoth of a sofa.

When I first met Moll Anderson, I had no idea how much she would color my world. She lives her own dazzling message of brightening up life with color, whether she's arranging dozens of yellow roses in a vase or applying a touch of teal eyeliner to enhance her soulful eyes. Moll inspires me to be brave. Against my every instinct, I bought the curvaceous lavender velvet sofa that afternoon, and the spell it had cast over Moll immediately took hold of me. That one improbable, impractical decision triggered what proved to be an important transformation in my life. I had somehow introduced not just a new piece of furniture into my space but a soft, new energy into my entire being. The sofa commanded a new, pastel palette: out went my familiar green, orange, and brown accents, and in came soft, feminine purple, silver, and pink tones. My day-to-day outlook felt light and fresh.

That crazy purple sofa is a symbol of gentle change for me, bearing testimony to a certain time and mood, and the shift to an unabashedly feminine chapter of my life story. It's a statement piece in every sense of the word. Some things that we bring into our homes not only reflect our style; they reflect our souls. Color doesn't merely say something *to* you—it says something *about* you. I never knew I loved lavender until I lived with it, and I never knew I needed lavender until Moll said so.

I used to be a black and white and neutral kind of girl, attracted to and comfortable in the earth tones of the Arizona desert where I grew up. It wasn't until Moll introduced me to one of our favorite artists that I entertained the possibility of bright, neon colors living on my great-room wall. At first I thought the art was adolescent and resembled a scribbled chalkboard. Now I bask in the childlike ambiance and playful mood that detail brings into my home.

Color speaks to all of us in many ways, often subtle and even silent. It isn't about the perfect décor, nor is it about choosing just any color of paint to match your décor. Color is about where you find your happy place, and what mood it inspires in your life. Finding the right fit is important, but what sets Moll apart is her uncanny way of getting you to let your color guard down, to open yourself up to the surprise and delight of unexpected revelation.

Moll's guidance and exercises will help you discover what tones can help design the space of your dreams. Moll has now captured colors beyond the rainbow and defines them in a language that we can see and feel. She represents all colors to me—even ones I never knew, until now. If you are ready to stop living in black and white and color your personality, this book will help you find the perfect tone.

Brooke Burke-Charvet

I am so excited to share the next phase of *Change Your Home, Change Your Life*™ with you—and this time, it's all about color!

I've always believed that our homes and environment are a direct reflection of what goes on inside of us. It has been ten years since *Change Your Home, Change Your Life*™ first published, and I have enjoyed the life-changing conversations that have sprung up around it. Now I'm ready to expand the dialogue and take it to the next level! With this book, I'm going to help you discover your very own personal color story. Did you even know you had one? For a long time, I didn't.

If you knew you could change your life in one weekend and clear out the cobwebs of your past with color and a brush, would you do it? This isn't just DIY, this is an emotional shift, and with this book, I am going to give you a prescription of color.

Color is an amazing source of energy and has a sensory effect on all of us. It affects our moods, our feelings, and even our behaviors. Color is a language that can be used to express many things about you that aren't immediately expressed in words. Most people assume that when they look at a color, it's strictly a visual sense by using only their eyes to see. The truth is, when we look at a color, it's not just with our eyes; we take in color as a full sensory experience. That includes all our senses, our emotions, our experiences, and even our childhood memories, good and bad, right up until this very moment. Everything in your life plays a part in your color story. If it affected you, then it matters. It's your truth and it's your color story. In the same way that a memory can be something painful, it can also be the absolute opposite. It could be the happiest, most wonderful memory that makes you love a certain color.

COLOR IS AN AMAZING SOURCE OF ENERGY AND HAS A SENSORY EFFECT ON ALL OF US. IT AFFECTS OUR MOODS, OUR FEELINGS, AND EVEN OUR BEHAVIORS.

Have you ever actually wondered why you are drawn to certain colors, but have a strong dislike for others?

It wasn't until I started considering why I felt certain ways about specific colors and how they affected me, that I realized I had my very own color story. After some serious soul-searching, I discovered that I no longer preferred the colors that I had loved as a child, and then I realized I hadn't loved them since my childhood. Why? The joy I had

INTRODUCTION

experienced from these colors had come to an end without me even realizing it. When I looked a little deeper, I discovered that my love of color had been taken away from me because of some very painful things that had happened to me at that particular time. At the age of four years old, completely unrelated to my parents, I had experienced something traumatic at the hands of a family friend. My ability to process at that young age exactly what was happening to me was

THE TRUTH IS, WHEN WE LOOK AT A COLOR, IT'S NOT JUST WITH OUR EYES; WE TAKE IN COLOR AS A FULL SENSORY EXPERIENCE.

beyond my comprehension. So I went to a safe place in my head and heart, similar to shock. Because I was unable to deal with it, I stuffed it away inside and at that moment began to withdraw and to hide. Similar to when one closes the drapes or crawls under the covers, I began to gravitate toward colors that were dark and safe. Colors that I once loved, like bright, fun yellow and hot pink, were now a problem; I associated them with explosions of feelings that I could not control,

and the painful memories I did not want to think about. As I grew older, without even realizing it, I started to decorate with darker colors, which felt warm and safe, cocoon-like. They were deeper tones, like black, gray, and olive. These colors are beautiful in themselves, but it wasn't until a couple decades later that I began to hunger for answers as to what happened to my love of vibrant color. Although I attempted to brush it off, assuming that maybe I had "grown up" and now liked more "sophisticated" colors, I couldn't shake the feeling that there was more to it than that. I was starting to realize that my aversion to those cheerful, bright hues that I used to love was so much deeper than simply disliking certain colors.

As this new awareness struck me, I started to notice that this personal interaction with color was not unique to me; it affected not just me personally but also friends and clients—especially when decorating their homes. Clients would say, "I absolutely love cobalt blue, but whatever you do, don't use red anywhere." Or, "I want a house that's fun and bright, like lime green and orange. Please do not use any dark colors at all!" With friends, I've always considered the importance of knowing their likes and dislikes, especially regarding color, when buying gifts. Even when people are dating, the "what's your favorite color?" question seems to come up.

Think back to your very first bedroom that you can remember. Most of us as children did not get to choose the color of our bedrooms or the bedroom furniture and linens. We basically start off living with the color memories of our parents and what they have chosen for us because of their own color stories and what they have learned and believed to be the preferred color choices for us as children. Often when parents have negative associations with certain colors from their own childhood, they will gravitate away from those colors for their children. I recently had a conversation with a young mother who considered herself as a child to be a tomboy, but her parents wanted her to dress more like a girl and forced pink and girly colors on her. This caused pink to become a negative color to her. Later, when she was pregnant with her first child, who happened to be a girl, her color story came into play when selecting the hues of the nursery. She was determined not to do to her daughter what her parents had done to her, so she chose more ambiguous colors, decorating the nursery in shades of purple and blue. But when she recently asked her preschool-aged daughter what she would like to wear that day, her daughter excitedly and joyfully blurted out, "Mommy, I want to wear pink; I just love pink!" Now this mommy is surrounded by a sea of pink everywhere she turns, and it's just fine with her.

Whether you loved your childhood room or disliked it, what plays a part in how you feel about your room from way back then? That's simple; it's the life you lived growing up in that space—as a matter of fact, in your entire home. And although your surroundings have influenced why you lean toward or away from certain styles as well, it's all about color. Color is energy—good or bad depending on your personal color story. If your childhood is a warm and happy memory, then you may tend to love the colors in your childhood room and home and feel safe in those hues. However, if you had any trauma, unhappiness, illness, or severe stress in those spaces, you may have shut down to color or have a strong aversion to certain colors that remind you of that time.

INTRODUCTION

When I was young, I took piano lessons from a very sweet older woman whose home smelled like cigarettes and mothballs. The piano room was actually a lovely pale blue and well organized, but the effects of the odors made me nauseous and even gave me headaches. As a matter of fact, they were so strong that the scents lingered on my clothes long after I left. I dreaded going back every single week. For years, every time I saw that pale shade of blue, my sense memory would kick in, and before I understood how I got there, I subconsciously decided I disliked that color.

I have met so many people who have shared details with me about their lives and

ARE YOU READY FOR A CHANGE?

homes, which easily opened up my ability to answer those questions I had about color and the effects it has on us. This research has become a part of my normal, everyday routine because the topic seems to naturally come up. For instance, on a recent photo shoot, I walked into the room wearing a very vibrant orange coat. Immediately, a gentleman blurted out, "Oh my gosh, that's bright!" and stated that he hated orange. Being the color lover that I am now, and because I'm on this journey, I had to ask why he felt this way. He said he actually hated it so much he had decided at a very young age to avoid the color orange and had managed to evade the color up until now, in his late fifties! After questioning him further, I learned that his father—whom he loved very much—always wore a certain hue of orange that was very attention grabbing. His father apparently loved being noticed and this bothered the man as a little boy. This realization started bringing his color story together that very day. And by the end of the shoot and after talking about it, he actually commented that he was open to the possibility that maybe orange deserved another chance in his life, especially the hue I was wearing. Progress in action!

I love hearing people tell me about their personal color stories, which most of the time they hadn't even realized they had.

So what about my color story? Well, let me start with one of my favorite quotes: "You don't get rid of yesterday by talking about it

all the time." I say you get rid of its negative effects on you by writing or painting the words on a wall—giving visual life to the pain in a color that allows you to take action and helps you move forward.

So I took my own words to heart and let go of things that had caused me years of pain. Don't get me wrong; it was a long process over many years—until I was 45

WHEN YOU ARE FILLED WITH ENERGY AND JOY, SO IS YOUR HOME.

years old—but only because I didn't realize that I had the power to take control of my home and life. It was time to stand on my own two feet and fight for me to become who I was always meant to be.

This change is first mental, and then you must take a physical action by writing the words down and reading them out loud so that you can really grasp that this thing or painful memory you are holding on to is such a waste of your energy and life. When you let go of pain, your heart and mind open up, and this allows you to have space to refill your mind, heart, and soul with joy and energy! It's so exciting and transforming, and it begins to free you to finally live the life that you were always meant to live. When you are filled with energy and joy, so is your home.

INTRODUCTION

On my walls I chose to paint and roll away all the stuff I was holding on to. For me it was simple: forgiveness toward people and things that had hurt me, but more important, forgiveness and compassion for me, that little girl who used to love color with all her heart.

ROLL AWAY THE OLD AND BRING IN THE NEW!

For that girl whose voice was taken from her because she couldn't tell. She couldn't speak up. She was emotionally paralyzed and learned how to go to that safe place in her head because she couldn't scream out for help. I wrote it in paint on my wall and I lived with it a couple of days, saying it out loud over and over. I went so far as to lock the door and put up a barricade as a "room in progress" so my son and the rest of the family wouldn't see it. I then started painting over it, visualizing it as if it were a sludge-like substance and I could see it leaving with all my pain. I physically and emotionally began to let it go. I cried so deeply, declaring out loud and thinking of Gandhi's quote, "No one can ever hurt me without my permission." Not only did I begin to feel lighter, but I started to laugh as this color took over the darkness of my life and brought newfound peace and joy into it. I was also becoming bright and fun and my wall was starting to look pretty awesome as well. And just like that, I was once again living in color.

For you, it may be as simple as saying goodbye to the negativity that surrounds your life and your home. Whatever you need to do to let go, do it; you can write a whole wall's worth of stuff if you need to. And then comes the good part—the fun part— race to the paint store and pick out that color that will breathe new energy into your space, and say goodbye to those heavy old thoughts by rolling away the old and bringing in that new color that makes your heart race and skip a beat or makes you want to dance! Sound too simple? Anytime you visualize a new beginning and take action, you can make it happen.

Are you ready for a change?

Inside this book I give you the keys to help you open up your senses and unlock your color story—your own personal connection to color. Thirteen color sections will ignite your creativity and motivate you to invite color into your home and life. Five fearless ideas will give you the courage to move forward. And when you're finished, your home and life will be filled with healing color.

I hope you will continue with me on this fun and introspective journey because you *do* have a color story!

We all have them, and it's so exciting to watch others come alive as they begin to put together all the pieces of their personal color stories. So come on, *Change Your Home, Change Your Life*™*...with Color!*

moll

HEARTBREAK
LOSS
FEAR
CONTROL
GUILT
ABUSE
HUMILIATION

MAKING SENSE

OF COLOR

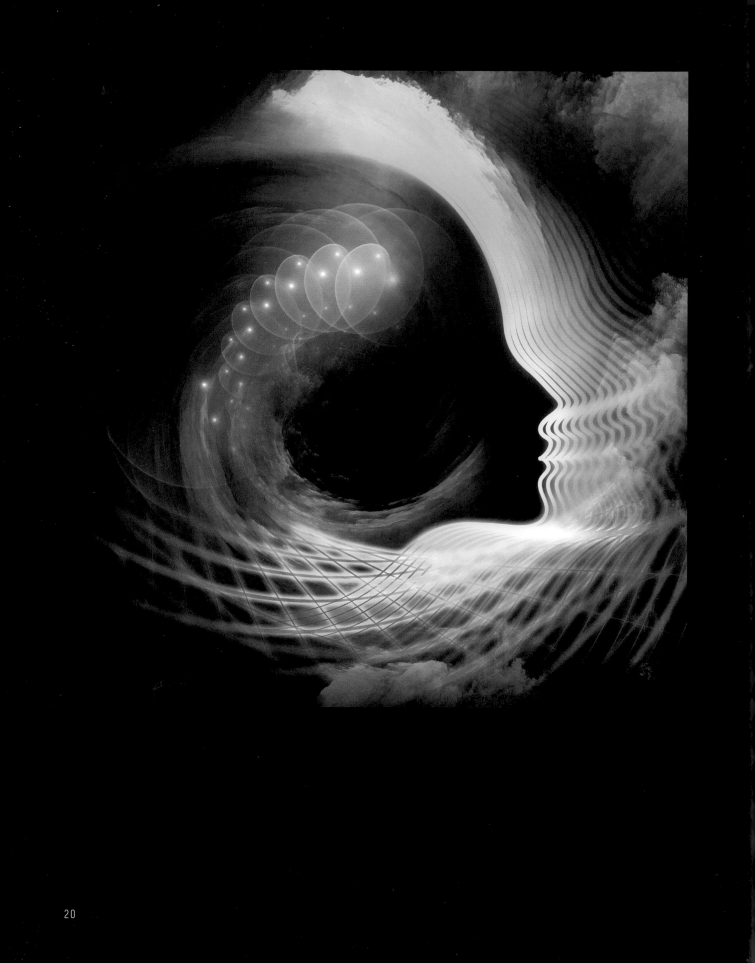

THE KEY TO
UNLOCKING
YOUR COLOR SENSE

SIGHT, SOUND, SMELL, TASTE, AND TOUCH—
IT'S TIME TO COME TO YOUR SENSES!

Sense memory plays a significant part in who we are today. In fact, it's so important that it's among the very first lessons we are taught. Long ago, in kindergarten, we all learned about our five senses. You may remember the pictures of an eye, ear, nose, mouth, and hand on your grade-school worksheet. It all seems pretty basic, but it's truly important to understand how things work as a child. Watch closely, and you'll notice children respond to color in such an honest, open way. When they love a color, it's obvious, and they choose a favorite very quickly. They are open to color because they're connected to their senses and attuned to how the color makes them feel. The thing is, we tend to forget later in life just how precious those senses are. We get caught up in our daily lives, distracted by the busyness and stress of work and family. We take for granted the importance of just how amazing our senses are to help us to enjoy life until we meet someone who has lost their hearing or ability to taste, or who was born blind and has never seen the beauty of the world around them. Luckily, our senses are so powerful that if we lose any one of them, all the other senses step up to help us function and learn a different route to our most necessary sensory experiences. These five simple but extraordinary abilities are truly gifts from God. Being in tune with your senses can change the way you live.

EXPLORING YOUR COLOR MEMORIES

Your feelings about color are deeply rooted and emotionally based on your own life. Therefore, making sense of how you feel about color is the first step and a very important key to exploring your color memories.

Starting with your home and family, and then moving on to the people who surrounded you growing up, like teachers, babysitters, and coaches,

consider all the influencers in your life. These influencers have played a significant part, from early childhood until this very moment! Because we carry our memories both consciously and subconsciously, we often need help sparking those memories,

which can be done by looking at old family movies or pictures, remembering favorite toys and dolls, and connecting with family and childhood friends. As you start to connect with your memories of colors and life, sift through them mentally and emotionally, holding on to the good memories and letting go of the bad ones, so you can move forward and create new ones!

COLOR MEMORIES HOLDING YOU BACK

Color is a powerful influencer, and the way we feel when we see a color we dislike can affect us physically. We may suddenly feel exhausted, anxious, or angry, and although we may not understand why, it's definitely a strong aversion. You may have known you hated the color, but didn't realize that the color was actually adding to your anxiety. For instance, when you enter someone's home for the first time and notice the entire room is painted in a color that you have an aversion to, it could negatively influence the way you interpret the visit. However, when you come into contact with a favorite color you love, you may begin to feel energy, excitement, or even calm.

Perhaps you have a favorite boutique where you love to shop and you always feel great being there. If that's the case, consider the color of the walls. Or maybe the colorful fashions add cheerful fun into the space, making you feel like a kid again. Whatever it is, being there makes you feel good.

Not all color and life memories are bad, and it's important to tap into both as you discover your color story.

I've provided some simple and fun questions throughout the book to start you on this journey, but don't stop there; when a memory comes to mind, or you remember something from a dream, write it down in a journal. It could be a key to discovering your color story and not allowing your color memories to hold you back anymore!

SENSORY STATE OF MIND

When we live attuned to our senses, we are more able to live a full sensory experience. We will look at everything differently. This state of mind will influence how we spend time inside our homes, outside in our yards, and

EVERY COLOR CHOICE WILL CONTRIBUTE TO THE VITALITY AND VIBRANCY IN YOUR DAILY LIFE.

even in our office spaces. It will change how we exercise and dine, how we choose our wardrobe, our makeup, our music, even our automobiles. Every color choice will contribute to the vitality and vibrancy in our daily lives.

Using our senses to the fullest is essential for experiencing this exciting world that we've only dreamed of creating. Your life and your home will completely transform and come alive. How will you know when this is happening? First, you'll develop an awareness of color

around you, becoming conscious of how it affects you. You may start to crave color; for instance, you might become enamored with a brilliant blue sweater you see in a store window. Perhaps you walk into a home furnishing shop to buy a practical, neutral-colored sofa but find yourself drawn to a red one. Maybe you come across a picture of a bedroom in different shades of purple and find yourself wishing you were daring enough to create that in your own space. By living in a sensory state of

mind, when color inspiration strikes, you will be completely aware and ready to welcome the color that you're so passionate about. Once you open yourself up to sensory living and incorporate color into your life, you will begin to truly appreciate just what you've been missing. It is the powerful result of understanding your very own color story. Your whole world will open up as you embrace the color that will energize and revamp your home.

Color is the one element in home and design that I refuse to live without because of the way it brilliantly adds "wow" and creates a sensory experience. As you explore your own color story, there will be many ways to introduce color into your home and life.

Color is so much more than just aesthetics. It allows you to create exactly the right atmosphere based on the emotional needs and behaviors of you and your family. Consider what your emotional reaction is to a certain color. Will it affect your behavior in a positive or negative way? How does it affect others living in that space? Remember, everyone has his or her own color story. If someone in your family has a strong aversion to a color, you won't create the peaceful, warm, and inviting environment you desire. Compromise might be needed if there are opposing responses to a certain color. Determine what colors work well for everyone in your home, and search for a balance that will create a loving, positive sensory environment.

WHAT'S YOUR COLOR STORY?

1. WHAT IS YOUR FAVORITE COLOR? WHY DO YOU LOVE THIS COLOR?

_____
_____
_____
_____

2. WHEN DID YOU DISCOVER THAT YOU LOVED OR HAD A PREFERENCE FOR THIS COLOR?

_____
_____
_____
_____

3. WHAT WAS YOUR FIRST ENCOUNTER WITH YOUR FAVORITE COLOR? WAS IT AN OBJECT, A PIECE OF CLOTHING, A PAINT COLOR, A ROOM, OR IS IT FROM AN EXPERIENCE?

_____
_____
_____
_____

4. DID YOU HAVE A MOST USED CRAYON IN THE BOX? IF SO, WHAT COLOR WAS IT?

_____
_____
_____
_____

5. WHAT MEMORY FROM CHILDHOOD DO YOU ASSOCIATE WITH YOUR FAVORITE COLOR? HOW OLD WERE YOU IN THIS MEMORY?

_____
_____
_____
_____

6. HOW DO YOU FEEL WHEN YOU EXPERIENCE YOUR FAVORITE COLOR? WHAT EMOTION DOES THIS COLOR EVOKE?

_____
_____
_____
_____

7. WHAT IS YOUR LEAST FAVORITE COLOR? WHY DO YOU DISLIKE THIS COLOR?

_____
_____
_____
_____

8. WHEN WAS THE FIRST TIME YOU NOTICED YOU HAD A STRONG DISLIKE FOR THIS COLOR?

_____
_____
_____
_____

9. HOW WAS THIS COLOR USED? WAS IT AN OBJECT, A PIECE OF CLOTHING, A PAINT COLOR, OR IS THIS A COLOR MEMORY FROM AN EXPERIENCE?

_____
_____
_____
_____

10. HOW DOES IT MAKE YOU FEEL WHEN YOU EXPERIENCE THIS COLOR?

_____
_____
_____
_____

IT'S ALL ABOUT
HUE

WHICH HUE IS FOR YOU?

Color is the most important design element when setting the mood of your space, so it's important to consider how your choices will affect the way you live and how you enjoy your home. Because color appeals to your emotions, when selecting a color palette, you need to think beyond design aesthetics, and get in touch with how the colors you choose make you feel. Some colors will energize and excite you, while others will make you feel anxious and depressed; some will be soothing and calming, and others warm and inviting. Color is a personal choice, but in selecting the colors for your home, there are a few things you need to know before you start. The colors you choose work together to set the mood of your space. For example, if you love the calming effects of blue but you pair it with a vibrant yellow, the energy in your space will change. The color orange may be your color of choice for creating a sunny, happy space, but when used in combination with gray, the mood will be different than when orange is used with a hot red or a deep blue. Colors also change their energy based on their darkness or lightness and saturation of the color. A lighter tint of a color will soften the tone and make a space feel larger and brighter; darken the color and your room will appear smaller and more intimate. When color is saturated, the vibrancy of the hue will bring more energy to your space. With an endless variety of tints, shades, and tones, how do you decide which hue is for you?

PAINT YOURSELF OUT OF A CORNER

It's easy to find yourself lost in the paint department, completely overwhelmed by the number of options to paint your walls. Perhaps you have stared, frustrated, at the aisles of paint swatches, hoping one will jump out at you and scream, "Take me home!" You are not alone! Trust me—we have all been there. Choosing the perfect paint colors can be overwhelming when offered a sea of so many beautiful choices. When I first started my career in Nashville, Tennessee, I spent hours at a time in the paint department of the home improvement store. After quickly determining what colors I needed, I would linger, giving advice to people in need of Prescriptions of Color™.

There they were, completely dazed and confused about what colors would be best for their homes and their lives. I even resolved a few family squabbles by intervening when I saw trouble brewing over who was going to win the argument regarding their color choice. Many people were decorating their first home; others were expecting babies and were looking for the perfect color for the nursery; some were struggling with divorce—wanting a fresh, new start. Some had lost a loved one and felt a need to embrace a new beginning alone. I loved helping them all, and I really love helping you now! I'm here to guide you along in this discovery of your exciting color story. But remember, you hold the key to finding your true hue so that you can paint yourself out of whatever corner life has you in. What are you waiting for?

COLOR VIBE
The color you paint your walls can affect your mood and emotions. Choose colors that bring the vibe you want to your space.

In beginning your color journey, paint color is extremely important in creating your new environment. When choosing a paint color for your walls, don't assume the color you see at the store will look the same in your own space—your unique lighting makes a difference. The amount of light in your room will affect how colors appear. If you have little natural light, the colors will seem darker; abundant natural light will cause the colors to appear lighter. The presence or absence of light in a space can brighten or soften a color, or change the hue entirely.

Test your color in both lighter and darker shades on a wall in your room to see how it's affected by light at different times during the day. This will allow you to adjust the color before painting the entire room.

UNDERSTANDING YOUR COLOR LANGUAGE

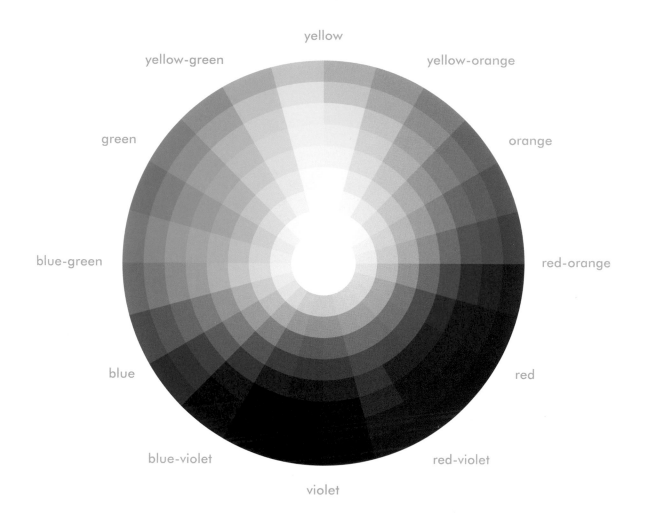

yellow

yellow-green

yellow-orange

green

orange

blue-green

red-orange

blue

red

blue-violet

red-violet

violet

PRIMARY COLORS

The primary colors of red, yellow, and blue are pure colors and cannot be formed by mixing any other color. Mixing these primary colors in different combinations creates all the other colors of the color wheel.

SECONDARY COLORS

Orange, green, and violet are secondary colors formed by mixing equal parts of two adjacent primary colors. Mix red and yellow to make orange, blue and yellow to make green, and red and blue to make violet.

TERTIARY COLORS

These colors are formed when mixing a primary color with a secondary color next to it. All the tertiary colors have a two-word name, such as yellow-orange, blue-green, and red-violet.

BECOME A COLOR EXPERT

To become your own color expert, you will need to familiarize yourself with the color wheel, which is an essential tool for helping you to mix and match colors and see the relationships between them. But remember, it is all about you finding the color that speaks to your senses and brings joy to your home.

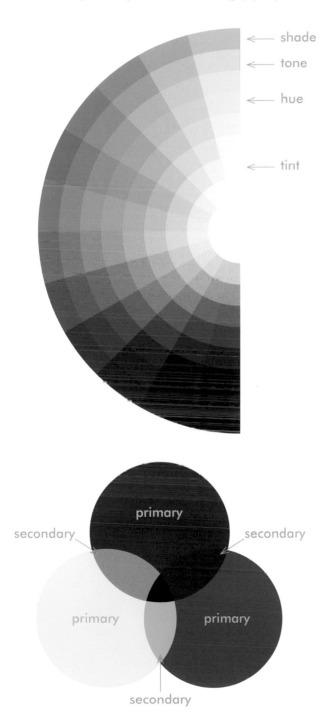

← shade
← tone
← hue
← tint

primary
secondary
secondary
primary
primary
secondary

COMPLEMENTARY COLORS

These colors are opposite each other on the color wheel and work well paired together. They complement each other, creating maximum contrast that makes each color appear brighter when they're used together. The three pairs of complementary colors are yellow and violet, blue and orange, and red and green.

HUE

Hue is the family of all the colors, the full spectrum of colors on the color wheel, including the primary, secondary, and tertiary colors. *Hue* is another name used interchangeably with the word *color*.

THERE ARE THREE WAYS TO ALTER THE COLORS ON THE COLOR WHEEL.

TINT

Add any amount of white to a color and it becomes a tint. Colors can be slightly tinted or heavily tinted to nearly white.

SHADE

Add any amount of black to a color and it becomes a shade.

TONE

Any color with gray added becomes a tone.

① START SMALL AND PAINT A WALL—NOT THE WHOLE ROOM.

Consider painting an accent wall at the end of your hall, your family room, or your entry foyer. Paint is a budget-friendly way to experiment with color and enliven your space. Use color to highlight architectural features, add depth to the back of a bookcase or built-in, or bring drama to your ceiling. Or go big and explore the possibility of infusing color into your smallest spaces, such as a powder room, laundry room, or home office. And don't forget furnishings—breathe some new life into your old furniture and transform them into colorful accents. Paint is an affordable way to discover the perfect color for you. A little investment of your time and a can of paint is all you need.

② IF YOU CAN WEAR IT AND FEEL FAB IN IT, THEN YOU CAN LIVE WITH THAT COLOR!

It's all about hue! Start with the color you love to wear and mix your hues. Your favorite wearable color comes in many tones, tints, and shades, and your closet will often reveal that you are attracted to varying hues of the same color. Explore the possibility of bringing your favorite fashion color to your space by mixing lighter and darker tones in the same color family into your paint, fabric, and accessories. When mixing lighter and darker tones in a monochromatic color palette, you are creating a relaxing, balanced room. The mix of subtle tones and vibrant hues will create a mood-enhancing elegance in your space.

③ BE SMART, THINK ART.

Be inspired by your favorite piece of art. Art is a great way to personalize your space and bring color into your room. Find a painting you love, and let that be your inspiration for choosing your color palette. If you cannot afford to buy art, then create your own. Find a lithograph or a photo that you love and make it into a large-scale piece. Hang it with or without a frame. Find an artist who has a style that speaks to you, and paint a canvas with the colors you love in a modern vibe. You will be amazed at the impact a large-scale painting full of color can bring to your space. Flea markets and garage sales have long been a great source for unexpected finds and great inspiration.

FEARLESS FIVE

④ A POP OF COLOR GOES A LONG WAY!

Make a bold statement with colorful accents. Accessorize! It's an affordable way to infuse color into your room and space, with minimal risk. You can easily change the vibe by swapping out some key accessories. Choose your favorite color to infuse into your life in fabrics, pillows, draperies, or an accent rug. When it comes to the bathroom, go for brightly colored towels, robes, and bath mats. A simple folded throw over the arms of a sofa and a colorful tray or collection of books will pop color into any space in a flash.

⑤ FLOWER POWER YOUR WAY TO A BOUQUET THAT MAKES YOUR HEART SING.

Take home a bouquet and see how flowers arouse your senses. There are numerous places where you can pick up flowers that won't break the bank. A visit to a local wholesaler will offer a full sensory experience of the widest variety in one place—from the exotic to the simplest of daisies. Peruse aisles full of the most colorful blooming florals sure to get your heart racing. But don't forget your great neighborhood florists as well, and never discount your grocer, flower stands, and wholesale clubs. They are carrying well-priced flowers daily and are also willing to order your favorites. The idea is to try a new color of flowers every week until you connect to the color for you and your home that breathes new life into your space.

> "ANY WAY YOU LOOK AT IT, TRY ONE IDEA OR ALL AND YOU WON'T HAVE TO FEAR A COLOR TAKEOVER AGAIN. YOU WILL BE YOUR OWN COLOR EXPERT!
>
> —moll

COLOR
DISCOVERY

Ever think about how much fun it would be to change the vibe of your room simply by switching out your pillows and throws? To help you in your color discovery, I chose some great colors to show you just how simple it can be. You could change it up for all four seasons, or jazz it up for a party, or just go with whatever mood you happen to be craving in your space for your new and exciting color vibe.

WHAT'S YOUR COLOR STORY?

1. WHAT WAS THE DOMINANT COLOR IN YOUR CHILDHOOD HOME? WHAT EMOTIONS DOES THIS COLOR EVOKE? DOES THIS COLOR BRING POSITIVE OR NEGATIVE MEMORIES?

_____

_____

_____

_____

2. WERE YOU ABLE TO CHOOSE THE COLORS OF YOUR CHILDHOOD BEDROOM? IF NOT, IF YOU COULD HAVE CHOSEN YOUR BEDROOM COLOR, WHAT COLOR WOULD IT HAVE BEEN?

_____

_____

_____

_____

3. IF YOUR PARENTS WERE TO GIVE YOU SOMETHING PARTICULAR FROM THEIR HOME AND LIFE, WHAT WOULD YOU LOVE TO RECEIVE AND WHAT COLOR IS IT?

_____

_____

_____

_____

4. HAVE YOU KEPT ANYTHING SPECIAL FROM YOUR CHILDHOOD, AND IF SO, WHERE DO YOU KEEP IT AND WHAT COLOR IS IT?

_____

_____

_____

_____

5. HAVE YOU INCORPORATED YOUR FAVORITE COLOR INTO YOUR HOME? IF NOT, WHY NOT? ARE YOU AFRAID TO USE THIS COLOR IN YOUR HOME DECOR?

_____

_____

_____

_____

6. HAVE YOU GONE TO GREAT LENGTHS TO ELIMINATE YOUR LEAST FAVORITE COLOR FROM YOUR HOME AND LIFE?

_____

_____

_____

_____

7. HAVE YOU EVER CONSIDERED THAT IF A COLOR YOU DISLIKE HAD A MORE VIBRANT HUE OR A SOFTER TINT IT WOULD HAVE A DIFFERENT EFFECT ON YOU?

_____

_____

_____

_____

8. HAVE YOU EVER PAINTED YOUR WALLS A COLOR AND HATED IT? IF SO, DID YOU LIVE WITH IT, OR PAINT OVER IT?

_____

_____

_____

_____

9. DO YOU CHOOSE FURNITURE THAT IS NEUTRAL BECAUSE YOU ADORE NEUTRAL OR BECAUSE YOU'RE AFRAID OF COLOR?

_____

_____

_____

_____

10. DO YOU ADD ANY POPS OF COLOR TO YOUR ROOMS WITH ACCESSORIES? IF YOU HAVE ACCESSORIZED WITH COLOR, WHAT COLORS HAVE YOU ADDED AND WHY WERE THEY CHOSEN?

_____

_____

_____

_____

INSTA-
INSPIRATIONS

CAPTURE YOUR REAL-LIFE INSPIRATION Color inspiration can come from almost anywhere. Consider the images you have captured in your life, and use these to call attention to the colors that have surrounded you. What do your photo memories reveal? What colors and color combinations are you drawn to? Is there a common thread? Start capturing what speaks to you and use it later as inspiration to create something special. No longer are these just memories—now they are documented inspiration: **insta-inspiration**.

PRESCRIPTIONS
OF COLOR™

THERE'S SOMETHING ABOUT
COLOR

FIND YOUR COLOR CURE

One glance at these six colorful chairs and you know exactly which one you're going to run to and sit in. You don't have to think about it; it's an absolute connection with that specific color. It's happy and familiar. Wouldn't it be amazing if there was a color for each thing you go through in life, from disappointment to heartbreak to loss? What if you could get a "Prescription of Color" for exactly what you need to bring joy, healing, and energy into your home and life? You can start the process of change by physically rolling away negative heaviness with a can of paint and "color your world" toward the positive. Paint that depressing old room happy! Change the sadness you feel with a set of colorful new sheets. Put a skip in your step by adding some color to your wardrobe, or pick up a fabulous chair in a color that will excite you and revamp your living room. Maybe it's the addition of a colorful cocktail to your dinner party to cheer up your BFF.

What I'm proposing are simple "Pops of Color" for your home,
for your wardrobe, and for how you live your life. You don't have
to create rooms from ceiling to floor in the same color, unless, of
course, you want to. "Pops of Color" will get you thinking about just
how quickly and easily you can add a perfect dose of color to fix the
mood you've been stuck in and start living your life boldly. Because
trust me, there's just something about color

I GRIND
BUT
MORE
IMPORTANTLY
I PRAY

#TRANSFORMING BLACK & WHITE

moll's thought

A black and white space is the ultimate wow statement, taking the most contrasting of colors and creating a perfectly balanced room— the ying and the yang, the darkest of dark partnered with the lightest of light colors. I consider black and white to be the power color combo, not to be confused with the idea of living your life without color in a black-and-white world. The first televisions were thought to be in black and white, even the first photographs were considered black and white, but they were actually in grayscale. So yes, black and white make a fabulous duo.

Black and white, the most contrasting color combination, balances the power of black with the purity of white—the masculine and feminine. This combination expresses extreme opposites: night versus daylight, alpha and omega, salt and pepper. White's innocence complements black's sophistication. The use of black and white is the most design-friendly choice to start with because you can't make a mistake— it's either black or white. Black alone makes a powerful design statement, providing an anchoring element to your space. In contrast, white reflects light, making spaces appear larger. Together, this harmonizing duo gives a fresh, sophisticated, and dramatic look to your space.

Whether your look is contemporary, cottage style, or French country, black and white works well with any décor. An added benefit to this versatile combination is that black and white work well when paired with any accent color, from vibrant shades to softer pastels.

GETTING GROUNDED

When designing your home, shop for rugs early in the process. They are the foundation of your space and can add warmth to your room. Rugs also help to add the particular vibe and atmosphere you're trying to achieve. Your choice in flooring, whether wood, tile, stone, carpet, or concrete, forms the foundation for your space. Think about layering your room—that's where the rugs come in. A black and white and cream rug makes a bold yet fun statement in any space.

FLOWER *power*

The dynamic and delicate anemone, with its white, papery petals and contrasting black center, is increasingly popular as it makes for a modern or vintage vibe. These bold beauties add eye-catching interest when incorporated into large white bouquets or have a striking simplicity in small, low arrangements. Although they are not readily available year-round and typically fall in the more premium price range, some affordable alternatives are "Winter Queen" and "Kilimanjaro" Gerbera daisies. You can create a similar look by taking a white lisianthius and inserting a black scabiosa for a contrasting center. A couple of white blooms placed atop a bed of black river rocks in water also works well. There are no rules, so mix it up and have some fun—it's all about the complementary contrast you create with the bold combination of black and white.

#POP
OF COLOR

#DRAPES

Window treatments can immediately soften a room, and depending on the style of drapes you have, they can be hung in a variety of ways, from heavier drapes that puddle, to clean, modern drapes that just kiss the floor. Consider the style of your room and other colors used. Do you want solids and simple prints, or bold patterns? Heavy, traditional drapes, or light, airy panels? Also keep in mind the amount of sun that enters the windows—will you need fade-resistant colors and fabrics or lined panels to control the temperature? Custom draperies can be expensive, but fortunately there are many retailers who offer beautiful, affordable window coverings.

#BOOKS

This is one time it's important to judge a book by its cover! Books are a designer's best friend and are some of the easiest and most bountiful accessories around. Once you have your color palette in mind, start collecting books in those specific colors and tones and tuck them away. Look for particular books that go with collections you've already started and would love.

For a clean, modern vibe, wrap your books in paper of the same color. It's a fun and easy way to bring color into your space by using the books you already have. You can also pick some up inexpensively from yard sales or discount stores. Specifically look for old leather-bound books, which suit any style.

If your book collection is becoming an overgrown, unsightly mess on your coffee table, invest in floor-to-ceiling bookshelves and create an accent wall. Sort books by color and size to make a bold statement that becomes a work of art.

COLORFUL COCKTAIL

COCONUT VANILLA BEAN DREAM

1	vanilla bean
1/2 cup	water
1/2 cup	sugar
1/2 cup	coconut milk (full fat)
1 ounce	silver rum

Cut the vanilla bean down the center and scrape out the seeds. Make vanilla bean simple syrup by combining water, sugar, vanilla bean, and its seeds into a saucepan and bring to a boil until sugar dissolves. Remove the vanilla bean, leaving the seeds in the syrup. Chill thoroughly. Combine the coconut milk, simple syrup, and rum in a cocktail shaker with ice and shake until well chilled. Strain into a cocktail glass, garnish with a vanilla bean or orchid, and serve immediately.

#COLOR
LESSON

When our grandchildren come to stay with their GiGi and GrandDaddy in Dallas, this black and white guest room really pops with bright red. Black and white is the perfect color combination for a newborn, since babies begin their lives seeing only contrast and then bright, primary colors. In fact, the color red is the first color babies recognize, making hot reds and pinks the perfect colors for accessorizing a room that will bring your baby hours of joy and cooing!

When your nursery also doubles as a guest room, the sophistication of black and white stands strong and elegant.

The stuffed animals and toys can be removed temporarily, and pops of color can then come from flowers, pillows, or a throw.

To really pull this look together I used a simple set of matching white crib sheets and an infant-size pillow and duvet with added black trim to match the black pillow flange.

As your child or grandchild grows older, simple, inexpensive changes allow the room to grow with them.

NEWBORN BABIES CAN SEE ONLY IN BLACK AND WHITE, SINCE THEIR RETINAS CAN ONLY DETECT THE CONTRAST BETWEEN LIGHT AND DARK FOR THE FIRST SEVERAL WEEKS UNTIL THEY ARE ABLE TO SEE THEIR FIRST PRIMARY COLOR.

#COLORSTORY

When done right, pattern play can look so good and have a very fun and funky-sleek vibe. If you're dying to experiment with all kinds of fabrics, from bold to subtle design, then the combination of black and white is the best way to begin your dive into playing with pattern.

Start by collecting your favorite patterned black and white fabrics and sort them by similar textures, such as light, airy fabrics and heavier velvets. If you're on a budget, also sort your pieces into more expensive/less expensive categories. This will help you to be conscious of the cost of your fabrics, thus allowing you to choose wisely. Consider where you can afford a touch of the expensive fabric. For instance, a pillow is a great choice because it requires only a small amount of fabric but packs a punch of style. A chair covered in the more expensive fabric will make an affordable impact, as opposed to using a really expensive fabric in the drapes, which usually call for major yardage, causing the cost of your drapes to skyrocket.

When choosing any patterned fabric for drapes, it's important to gather and fold the fabric to get an idea of what visual pattern you will actually be seeing the majority of time when the drapes are open.

CREATIVE FIX

There are times when there really can be too much of a good thing, especially when it comes to bold patterns. My personal rule is to avoid repetition. The Greek key trim I chose and love for my throw pillows was a lock, so I struggled to find the right trim or braid for my drapes in this Florida room. Shifting direction, I searched for a fabric with a big, bold black-and-white pattern. However, the bold design was way too busy for the room as drapes, but when I cut and folded the fabric just right, it made the perfect trim, and was a creative fix. Sometimes too much *really is* too much, but you can use fabrics creatively to lessen their boldness.

COLORFUL TRIVIA

Their white coats with black stripes work together as camouflage when zebras stand in a group, making it harder for predators to determine how many there are. Just like our unique fingerprints, no two zebras' stripes are alike.

The top two greatest American movies of all time, according to the American Film Institute, are *Citizen Kane* and *Casablanca*, both in black and white. Out of the AFI's top ten ranking, four were shot in black and white.

The decision to use a black-and-white checkered flag at the start/finish line of an auto race came about because the high-contrast design makes it more visible to the drivers against the background of a crowd or dusty track.

Black and white patterns have been used throughout history to symbolize the balance and harmony between opposing forces, such as the yin-yang of Chinese philosophy, checkerboard floors in Masonic iconography, and the checked fabric used by the Balinese.

60

" WOMEN THINK OF ALL COLORS EXCEPT THE ABSENCE OF COLOR. I HAVE SAID THAT BLACK HAS IT ALL. WHITE TOO. THEIR BEAUTY IS ABSOLUTE. IT IS THE PERFECT HARMONY.

COCO CHANEL

#ENERGIZING ORANGE

The color of fire and sun, this brilliant color is a result of yellow's calming effects on red's aggression. Whether you choose the hot, fiery red-oranges; the fruity hues of tangerine, orange, apricot, or peach; or shades mixed with brown to create burnt orange, russet, or pumpkin, orange will revitalize your space with a warm, refreshing energy.

Since 2012, when Tango Tangerine was named, the Pantone Color of the Year, variations of orange have surged in popularity in home décor and fashion. From paint to makeup, home furnishings to accessories of all kinds, orange remains a popular color choice. A refreshing, stimulating, and positive hue, orange works well with other colors and can be used in combination with contrasting colors, or with soft gray, yellow, or bright white for a fresh, modern vibe. Energizing orange encourages, socialization, and creativity, releases warmth and positive energy, and creates a sense of playfulness and fun.

moll's thought

When I see orange I feel energy and want to dance! It wasn't always that way, I used to avoid orange at all costs. Perhaps my love of orange started with my love for my husband, Charlie, and his love of the University of Tennessee and their team color of UT Orange. Yes, love can often bring new meaning to a color! Sharing in a color can be a catalyst for change and a boost to your relationship. Give it a try.

TRAY CHIC

Little touches can transform any space into a warm and inviting home. Try adding trays in a variety of shapes, colors, and sizes. These can be the base for a small bouquet of flowers, colorful glassware, a book, or a tea set that welcomes guests to share a cup.

FLOWER *power*

#POP
OF COLOR

#ACCENT CHAIRS

Once you've made the decision to use furniture to add a pop of color to your room, a great chair is one of the best purchases you can make. As with any upholstery piece, a well-made chair can create many different vibes simply with a change of fabric. For example, this particular chair by "Shine By Sho" can be paired and nestled into just about any space. The energy of this shade of orange can brighten the start of any day.

Chrysanthemums come in a variety of shapes, sizes, and colors, making them a popular flower among florists. The flower of November, the chrysanthemum is generally regarded as a symbol of cheerfulness and positivity. Grouped together and paired with dahlias and accented with vivid foliage, winterberry, and other natural elements, mums become a focal point. Grouped together in shorter arrangements and divided among small water glasses, they are a simple way to add beauty to the center of a dining table.

#TABLE SETTINGS

Life offers so many occasions and opportunities to express yourself with your dinnerware. Whether family heirlooms, thrift store finds, or major splurges, dishes are a fabulous way to bring color into your life and the lives of your family and friends. Fortunately, table settings can include everything from mismatched flea market pieces to perfectly coordinated complete sets, making setting a table a no-stress event. And you'll never go wrong with a great set of all-white dishes as a foundation, bringing in color with flowers, food, napkins, or tablecloths. Build your dinnerware collection like you do your wardrobe—with good-quality staples and lots of fun, colorful additions. Before you know it you'll be mixing and matching like a party planning pro.

COLORFUL COCKTAIL

CITRUS HABANERO MARGARITA

1	habanero pepper
1/2 cup	freshly squeezed orange juice
2 ounces	silver tequila
	Kosher salt for the rim
	Orange slice for the rim

Slice the habanero pepper and remove its seeds. Place the sliced pepper in the orange juice and muddle to release the heat from the pepper. (Reserve one habanero slice.) Strain the spicy orange juice and combine with tequila. Take a slice of orange and rub it around the rim of the glass, and dip the rim into kosher salt. Fill glass with ice and pour the margarita over top. Garnish with a slice of orange and a thin habanero slice.

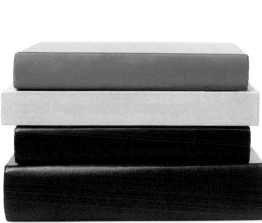

#COLOR
LESSON

Perhaps your space is like my Dallas kitchen: sleek, strong, and sophisticated. Consider introducing color in an organic way. Start by adding separate bowls of lemons, oranges, and limes, which are used in everyday life. Flowers, of course, are a must-have; yellow tulips and orange roses make even a room without windows feel sunny.

Marking an entryway into rooms is key to adding a touch of fabulous. These two modern orange suede stools create a wonderful boost of energy as you enter the kitchen.

To give stools or chairs an artistic purpose, add books with fun, bright covers and top with fresh flowers. Consider spraying succulents with a florescent paint for an energetic vibe with a long-lasting punch of color.

DON'T FORGET THE LIGHTING! SPARKLING CRYSTAL SCONCES CAN ADD TO THE PIZZAZZ WHILE LIGHTING THE WAY!

#COLORSTORY

ORANGE CRUSHING

There is nothing like hosting a party! Some of the most fun in planning a party is choosing the theme, which means working with a color you've been crushing on. This party was a summer soirée to honor my girlfriends as "goddesses" at the beach in Malibu. It called for all-white attire; the color was provided by headdresses, tablecloths, and the ribbons on my party favors.

The tablecloth set the foundation for the atmosphere—a Bohemian feel, but still sophisticated. When hosting, consider renting the linens, which allows you to choose something unique and fun without it becoming an investment. Whimsy is important when entertaining, and it's nice to have a surprise in store for guests. A headpiece of mixed orange and white florals upon arrival made guests feel as though they were being crowned goddesses, adding to the magical atmosphere. Table flower arrangements in a combination of white orchids and crème roses balanced the all-white attire.

Party favors are always a must and don't have to be expensive or extravagant. A few of your favorite must-haves, carefully placed in a pretty gold box and topped with an orange bow, can double as a place card.

A LITTLE SPLASH GOES A LONG WAY

The key to creating long-lasting design that you won't tire of is to think classic with your basics. This Dallas office is strong and modern but is balanced with rich chocolate plaster walls that provide the perfect backdrop for adding bold splashes of color with accents that do not overwhelm. The art, simple florals, and succulents introduce color to the space.

State-of-the-art appliances and solid furnishings are the foundation for this Knoxville kitchen. The open glass display is the modern focal point of this kitchen, offering both form and function to display artistic serving pieces and colorful accents.

COLORFUL TRIVIA

The Chevy Camaro first appeared in the iconic Camaro Hugger Orange in 1969, and even today collectors are willing to pay premium prices for an original in this color.

Oranges, pumpkins, carrots, sweet potatoes, and even autumn leaves get their orange color from a type of photosynthetic pigment called carotene.

In ancient Chinese religion orange was the color of transformation, based on the interaction of red with yellow.

Safety orange is used for life jackets, life rafts, and highway safety signs and cones because it is most easily visible in dim light and against a water background.

Pressed orange peel produces an oil used in flavoring food and beverages, perfume and aromatherapy, and as an environmentally friendly cleaning agent. Gardeners also use orange peel to repel slugs.

#ENERGIZING ORANGE

"ORANGE IS THE HAPPIEST COLOR.

— FRANK SINATRA

This is your Monday morning reminder that you are powerful beyond measure, that you are capable of pretty much anything you are willing to work for, and that you could change your life today. unknown

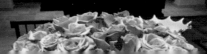

#INVIGORATING YELLOW

Uplifting, refreshing, and rejuvenating, yellow is a happy color strongly associated with the sun. Revered as a royal color linked to the sun god Apollo, the earliest yellow dyes were made from saffron, the world's most expensive spice. The vast spectrum of yellow hues provides many choices for your home, from creamy, buttery yellows to vibrant lemon and canary yellows, to deeper, muted shades of mustard, saffron, goldenrod, and butterscotch.

This highly reflective color will help to open up small spaces and bring light and warmth into those rooms that lack natural light. Use the creamy tones as neutrals, or pump up the volume with the more saturated lemon yellow. The deeper shades will add a timeless warmth and elegance to your home, creating a golden glow. An optimistic color, yellow raises spirits, instills hope, and releases a cheerful, positive energy.

moll's thought

Yellow makes me feel full of life and gives me energy! I keep bowls full of lemons in my kitchen to enjoy daily. The sun is so healing and its warmth always makes me feel happy and healthy. After losing my love of color, it was yellow that first revived me! Suddenly I was choosing yellow flowers, clothing, and furniture. I was drawn to it. Listen to your own heart and answer with color!

BRING THE WARM GLOW
OF SUMMER INSIDE

Once associated with hopeless love and jealousy, yellow tulips have made a sunny comeback in modern interpretations to stand for cheerfulness and friendship. Tulips naturally grow and stretch out in a vase, so select a vase that covers at least half the length of the stems. Keep these petals perky by changing the water and cutting the stems every other day, and by adding flower food, a penny, a little lemon juice, or cane sugar to the water.

#FAB FURNITURE

Unique pieces of fabulous furniture are like art! This includes any piece of furniture that is not typical of a space. Sometimes the color alone can make a very dull and basic piece exciting! This curved yellow settee placed in the middle of a room immediately causes a happening to stir. By adding a couple of comfy occasional chairs and a coffee table, you can create a cozy place to receive guests. Perfectly straight lines are not necessary when it comes to a sofa or chair. A curved piece is the perfect way to soften hard lines in a room.

To save space, a corner piece can have a unique look without dominating the room. Add an ottoman to the piece to give the illusion of a chaise. It will also allow extra seating when it's pulled away into the room.

#PILLOWS

Pillows—oh how I love them! Small ones, large ones—and most important, colorful ones! Pillows are a quick and easy way to add pops of color, introduce texture, and add visual interest to your rooms. They can easily and affordably be swapped, allowing you to change the look of your space whenever the mood strikes.

Pillows add a unifying element to your space. Choose colors, textures, and fabrics that either complement or contrast with your furniture upholstery or that are inspired by statement pieces such as art, a patterned rug, or draperies.

With so many options, it's important to choose the right ones to unify your space.

Pillow Talk
- Shapes and sizes: With such a range of sizes and shapes, including round, rectangular, bolsters, and squares, the pillow you select will depend on the size and scale of your furniture.
- Mix it up: A variety of shapes and sizes creates a more visually interesting "pillowscape."
- Fill 'er up!: Feather and down filling create a more comfortable plush feel and are more moldable, while the stiffness of foam and other fillers hold their shape.

COLORFUL COCKTAIL

BOURBON, LEMON & SAGE SPRITZER

¹/₂ cup	water
¹/₂ cup	sugar
6 leaves	fresh sage
1 ounce	bourbon
¹/₂ cup	freshly squeezed lemon juice
	Club soda

Make sage simple syrup by combining water, sugar, and the sage leaves in a saucepan and bring to a boil. Reduce the heat and let sit for 15 minutes. Strain and chill thoroughly. Combine the bourbon, lemon juice, and sage simple syrup in a cocktail shaker with ice and shake until well chilled. Pour over ice and top off with club soda.

When my husband and I decided to change our space, the first thing we did was knock down walls and bring in the light. We also wanted colorful modern art and fell in love with this fabulous painting. It had everything we wanted, especially the vibrant colors. We hung it up and knew it needed a bench with a major pop of color underneath it. I designed this bench inspired by a picture I had loved for years. The hardest part was deciding what color we wanted under this extremely colorful painting.

THE COUPLE "COLOR MERGE" EXERCISE

Making design decisions as a couple can be a challenge. But if you agree to work as a team, the reward will be worth it.

After choosing multiple fabric swatches to match the colors in your painting or inspiration piece, individually write down your first, second, and third choices. Read your choices aloud to see which ones you each picked. If your first choices don't match, it's okay! Discuss your preferences and choose from the other selections. If you can't agree, sleep on it. Try again later with a fresh perspective. If you still can't agree, then realize a compromise must be made. Sometimes metallics or neutrals can resolve this conflict.

> YOU AND YOUR PARTNER SHOULD BOTH LOVE THE HOME YOU CREATE TOGETHER. YOUR HOME SHOULD REFLECT WHO YOU ARE AS A COUPLE AND THE LIFE THAT YOU WANT TO LIVE.

#COLORSTORY

I love creating masculine spaces, so when I designed my husband's corporate offices in Knoxville, Tennessee, I was especially excited about doing his personal space. For this very special project I was inspired by one of his favorite suits and overcoat. The sofa is upholstered in gray flannel, the armchairs in a black with white pinstripe velvet/mohair. The carpet's mix of different tones of gray tweed and the coffee table's glass top and silver chrome base create a sleek and contemporary atmosphere.

The tonal palette of grays into black presented the perfect backdrop for whatever color was to be showcased. The finishing touches, like the large-scale painting, throws, and tulips, were the tie and the scarf of the "suit." Hot yellow once again won out in my color story! The strong gray and black tones ground the space and make a powerful statement, while the white balances and offers a bold contrast. This powerful combination is energized by the hot yellow that every man needs to brighten his business space.

COLORFUL TRIVIA

Pencils have been painted yellow since the 1890s, and still today, 75 percent of the pencils sold in the United States are yellow.

American school buses are painted yellow because the eye detects the color yellow the fastest, 1.24 times faster than red.

Yellow is the most visible color and is highly attractive to birds and insects, helping them to find mates and detect flowers.

Pigmented from clay, yellow was one of the first colors used in prehistoric cave art.

In Western cultures yellow has been associated with cowardice, but in the Chinese culture it is symbolic of heroism, happiness, glory, and wisdom.

When viewed from Earth, the sun appears yellow, but when viewed at a high altitude from space, it is actually white in color.

"I REALLY JUST WANT TO BE WARM YELLOW LIGHT THAT POURS OVER EVERYONE I LOVE.

CONOR OBERST

#INVIGORATING YELLOW

what you **think**, you **become**. what you **feel**, you **attract**. what you **imagine** you **create**.
—BUDDHA

THE MAP OF JAMAICA

MOLL ANDERSON
VIKKI KRINSKY

#BALANCING GREEN

Located in the center of the color spectrum, making it the color of balance, green combines the cool tones of blue with the warm tones of yellow. The cooler shades of jade, emerald, and Kelly green unite the elements of nature with the soothing blue tones of water and sky. The warmer, yellower tones of celadon, olive, and sage combine the warmth of the sun with balancing green. As nature's neutral, there is an abundance of green hues to choose, of which many are found in the natural world.

Known as a healing color, a touch of green added to every room will bring a natural balance and a healthy energy to your space. More than any other color, green appeals to the sense of smell, evoking the aromas of freshness and nature: a newly mowed lawn, the scent of lime, pine needles, mint, fresh herbs, and a refreshing spring shower. The color green not only represents health and healing; it also symbolizes balance and harmony, growth, renewal, and natural abundance.

moll's thought

Green introduced to a room naturally is my favorite kind of green and a must-have for balance. I love including fresh herbs, and am especially obsessed with mint and cilantro. They are the perfect additions when potted in the kitchen, ready to be picked at a moment's notice to add to a cocktail, cup of tea, or a fresh green salad. The aroma of fresh herbs fills the air and the color enlivens my kitchen, motivating me to cook up a storm.

SPRING INTO GREEN AND RUN WILD IN PINK

Tall oaks and magnolias cover the lush, rolling green hills of my Tennessee yard, enticing me to get outside and enjoy nature's beauty. Whether you have a yard, a terrace, or live in a high-rise condo in the city like my Dallas home, there are ways to add the healing effects of nature's green to your outdoor living space. Add planters, flower boxes, and trees to a small terrace, or even artificial grass to create a green landscape. Even the smallest bit of greenery to your outdoor space has healthy benefits.

Start by walking into the room and really taking a good look at it with fresh eyes; this will prepare you to edit the room. Then decide what really works in the space and which items seem out of place or uninteresting. Go with your immediate gut feeling, removing items quickly and putting them in a box to give away.

Be creative as you experiment with different staging ideas for your items until you fall in love with the vibe you've created. One of the most powerful sensory staging ideas is a monochromatic color scheme as seen here. Use objects with different heights to create a visual like you might see on display in a store.

"Sensory scape" is a term I coined many years ago when I first started my interior design career. I specialized in taking a very bland and boring room and resuscitating it back to life with carefully placed items! Many clients often called me to come over to revamp and renew their space using the accessories they already had. Whether they were looking to completely change the vibe, add one or two new items, or to finally introduce color into their space, I was the transformer!

TAKE A PICTURE OF THE ROOM YOU ARE HOPING TO REVIVE. A BEFORE PHOTO IS HELPFUL AS YOU CONSIDER THE DESIGN CHANGES. IT'S ALSO A GREAT WAY TO SHOW OFF YOUR WORK WHEN YOUR TRANSFORMATION IS COMPLETE!

FLOWER *power*

Of the carnation family, but with a unique look all its own, "Green Trick" dianthus is desired for its striking spherical shape, eye-catching fresh green color, and excellent vase life lasting up to four weeks. This modern bloom mixes in as filler for miniature arrangements or can be used like moss to create a focal feature by grouping blooms together. Playful, a touch whimsical, and simply chic, "Green Trick" is great for adding texture and color to any floral design.

#POP
OF COLOR

#OUTDOOR BENCH

There's nothing as inviting as a bench along a pathway that calls you to take a seat and enjoy the moment, letting you slow down to appreciate the beauty that surrounds you. But don't limit benches to the outdoors—there are so many fun ways to use them in your home. In an entryway, they offer a warm hello to guests as you welcome them into your home. In a large room, a backless bench can be used to divide the space without visually taking up too much room. A bench at the foot of a bed can be especially helpful when there's not room for a chair, and can double as a luggage holder. It's also a great way to add color!

#PLANTS

There are so many reasons to add beautiful living plants to your home. Besides adding lush and natural green layers into your space, plants add a sense of balance and are known to reduce stress, lower heart rate, and help us focus and relax. Whether you choose trees, leafy plants, or short grasses in containers, as seen here, make sure you take into consideration your lifestyle. If you're busy, choose low-maintenance plants, like cacti or succulents. Some plants require special watering and unique plant food, so consider this if you travel a lot. Before choosing the perfect plants for your home, assess the lighting in each space. Research your options, and then purchase your selections at a reputable nursery.

COLORFUL COCKTAIL

KIWI MOJITO

1 ounce	simple syrup (¹/₂ cup water and ¹/₂ cup granulated sugar)
10	mint leaves, plus more for garnish
1	kiwi, peeled and sliced, plus extra slices for garnish
1	lime, juiced
2 ounces	clear rum

Make simple syrup by bringing sugar and water to a boil. Turn off the heat and let the simple syrup chill completely. Muddle the mint leaves, kiwi slices, and lime juice in a cocktail shaker. Add the rum and simple syrup. Add 3 ice cubes and shake the cocktail shaker well until drink is completely chilled. Pour over crushed ice and add extra mint leaves, lime, and kiwi slices for garnish.

#COLORSTORY

I often hear, "What do I do with the space above the headboard?" When a tall bed shortens the space between the headboard and ceiling, should you fill the space or not? It depends on whether you feel something is missing. If so, then you probably need to hang something there. Trusting your gut instinct is important to discovering your design confidence.

The space above this headboard was screaming for design help. With a tight deadline, the mission was clear: I wanted a strong, sophisticated guest room that could switch from male to female energy depending on my guests. So this particular design was going to be all about color. I could then change out the pillows, sheets, and flowers to fit my needs.

I headed to the Dallas Design District and hit the galleries, where I instantly fell in love with this piece and its vibrant color.

Night vision goggles show images in green because the human eye is more sensitive to green and can detect the most shades of that color.

It has been reported that people with colorblindness can distinguish between different shades of green.

Originally, white medical scrubs were switched to green after one doctor suggested it would be easier on surgeons' eyes in the operating room, because green is opposite red on the color wheel.

Green is the rarest eye color of the human population, and is most common in Northern and Central Europe.

The back of the United States one-dollar bill has been green since 1861, the same year these US notes were nicknamed "greenbacks."

Billiards and game tables get their traditional green color as a representation of the grass lawns where our ancestors originally played the games.

"GREEN IS THE PRIME COLOR OF THE WORLD, AND THAT FROM WHICH IT'S LOVELINESS ARISES.

—————

PEDRO CALDERÓN
DE LA BARCA

Being negative
only makes a
difficult journey
more difficult.
You may be given
a cactus, but you
don't have to
sit on it.
—Joyce Meyer

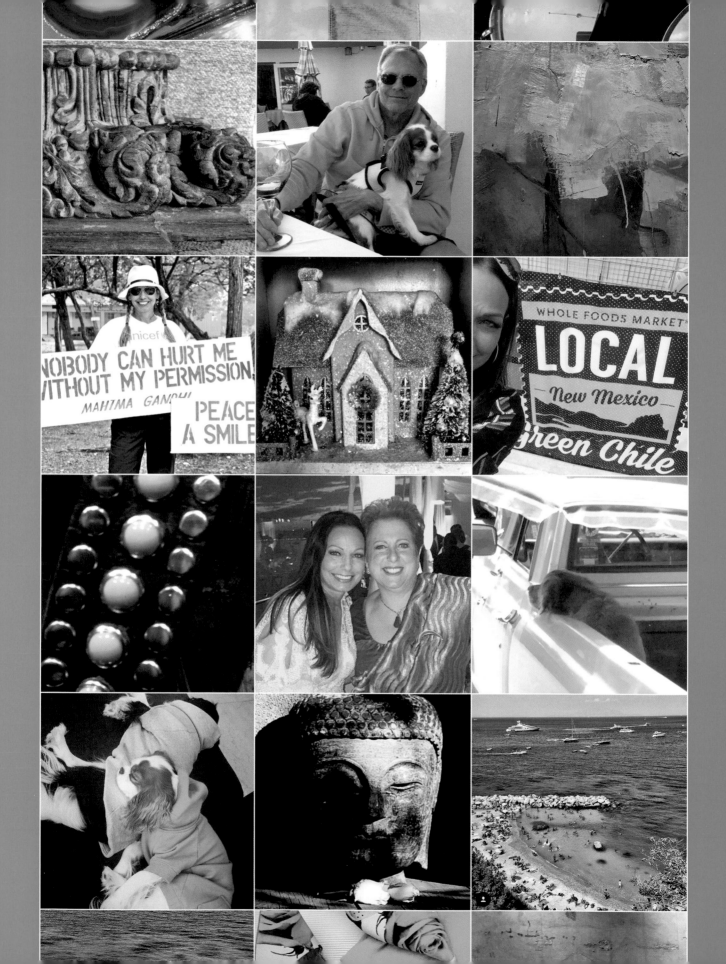

#REVIVING TURQUOISE

From the bright, invigorating aquamarine to the deeper warm tones of teal, turquoise is a modern and refreshing design choice for your home. Turquoise is a French word meaning "Turkish stone," from the gemstone of the same color. This bluish green hue combines the calming effects of blue and balancing effects of green, making it an attractive color choice in interior design.

Used in design throughout the ages, turquoise has found a place among ancient craftsmen, in their intricate mosaic designs, and among the Native American artistry of the American Southwest. From coastal cottage décor to contemporary interiors, turquoise is a captivating color to add to your interior design. Possessing the cool, soothing tones of the Mediterranean, the colors of turquoise and aquamarine bring the calming, rejuvenating serenity of an ocean breeze to your space. In color psychology, turquoise recharges your spirits, encourages emotional balance and healing, and creates tranquility and serenity.

moll's thought

What is it about turquoise that makes us feel like taking a deep breath and closing our eyes as we're transported to memories from our past? For me, it plops me right in the sand, my toes in the water, as I listen to the relaxing sound of the waves from the ocean, reminiscent of my childhood beach vacations and my memorable honeymoon in the luscious turquoise water of St. Bart's. Even years later, turquoise has the unique power to bring those special memories to the surface.

FLOWER *power*

#POP OF COLOR

#VASES AND BOTTLES

Colorful glass has a certain transparency that plays with the light in a flirty and fun way. Whether it's handblown or manufactured colored glass, you can't go wrong filling them with blooms or lining them up in a collection of rainbow colors on a shelf. Vintage, modern, and crystal—any kind of glass will do. Fill decorative glass bottles with bath salts, olive oil, and herbs or spices for a beautiful way to store those items.

If you're looking for an easy way to add some pizzazz to a table, the romantic look of old wine and Chianti bottles filled with long taper candles and dripping wax is sure to pump up the ambiance. Search antique shops and discount stores to start a colorful collection of glassware.

While Mother Nature provides a wide array of her most captivating colors in the form of flowers, there are relatively few shades of blue. Many of the brilliant turquoise blooms you see have been dyed to achieve that shade, but you can get that same look at home. The widely available Gerbera daisy is the perfect choice for coloring, as well as other white flowers—daisies, roses, hydrangea, and orchids—making it easy to create the perfect hue for you!

#TOWELS

There's something wonderful about walking down the aisles of the towel department and seeing colorful and beautifully folded towels. It's like a rainbow just waiting for you to pick up a new color—which does include white. While some people have never bought a set of white towels, others have never chosen a colorful set.

Since towels come in a wide price range, you don't need to be intimidated by the cost. Although most bath towels are made of cotton, they vary in their softness, absorbency, durability, and color-fastness, making fabric type an important feature. Whether you choose Egyptian or Pima cotton, they are both function and style rolled—or folded—all into one.

An armful of new towels can refresh and revamp your bathrooms. Stacked on a bathroom shelf, rolled in a basket by your tub or shower, or layered on a towel bar, towels add a colorful twist to your décor. Arrange by color and mix your hues. For a creative and modern touch try using three different shades of one color to give you an ombre effect.

COLORFUL COCKTAIL

SEA GLASS PUNCH

1 1/2 teaspoons	Blue Curaçao
2 ounces	rum
4 ounces	pineapple nectar
1/4 cup	fresh lime juice
Dash	nutmeg
	Sparkling water
	Pineapple leaves, for garnish
	Lime wedges, for garnish

Combine the Blue Curaçao, rum, pineapple nectar, lime juice, and nutmeg in a cocktail shaker with two ice cubes. Shake well until thoroughly chilled. Pour over two glasses filled with crushed ice to mimic the look of sea glass and top off with sparkling water. Garnish with pineapple leaves and lime wedges.

#COLOR
LESSON

Paint, plaster, or wallpaper can transform a small, boring room in an instant! This pass-through in our Dallas apartment was dark and not very exciting. While remodeling the space, Charlie and I took down the shelves and opened it up. With lots of imagination and myriad color samples, it went from boring and forgettable to a focal point and conversation starter.

Although plaster is a wonderful choice for this type of wall design, you can achieve the same look simply by using your inspired colors in paint and covering it with a shiny, clear polyurethane finish.

Wallpaper is bigger and better than ever! Explore how you're going to use the space, and then choose a paper that fits the mood. Remember that if you want to make a bold statement—think big, even in small spaces.

Use a small space to create a cozy place to connect with a loved one. I included two chairs, covered in a shiny vinyl to reflect more light, and a small table and beautiful chessboard.

PAINTING, DRAWING, AND COLORING ARE FANTASTIC WAYS TO BOOST YOUR CREATIVITY AND YOUR CONNECTIONS TO COLORS. USE PAINTS, COLORFUL PENCILS, AND MARKERS AND LET YOUR IMAGINATION RUN WILD!

#COLORSTORY

Sometimes the best design ideas come from allowing a space and color to speak to you.

The color palette of entrancing depths of exotic teals and midnight blues with hints of brilliant turquoise captivated me and drew me in to this beautiful painting by artist Michael David. The artwork was even the right scale at 74" x 86". This was a piece I needed in my home. However, positioning it on the wall horizontally did not work in our space, nor did hanging it vertically. After some thought and consideration, it struck me that what I loved so much about this painting was the brilliant turquoise color that I craved. The solution was two narrower paintings on either side of the original, bringing more splashes of turquoise into the space. Not only does it look amazing but it introduces the vibrant color I love, making this one of our favorite rooms.

CREATIVE FIX: If you're budget-minded, purchase three canvases with boxed edges in the sizes that work for you and order them three inches deep. Find a painting

that inspires you and, using acrylic paint or pastels, or even spray paint, use big, bold strokes to transform your canvas. The good news is that if you mess up you can paint over it, adding some great texture.

PILLOWS AND ACCESSORIES: The two pillows and a lacquer box in my inspired turquoise color, and the three back pillows in a fabric influenced by the color vibe of the painting, bring unity to the space.

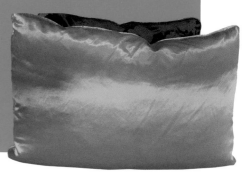

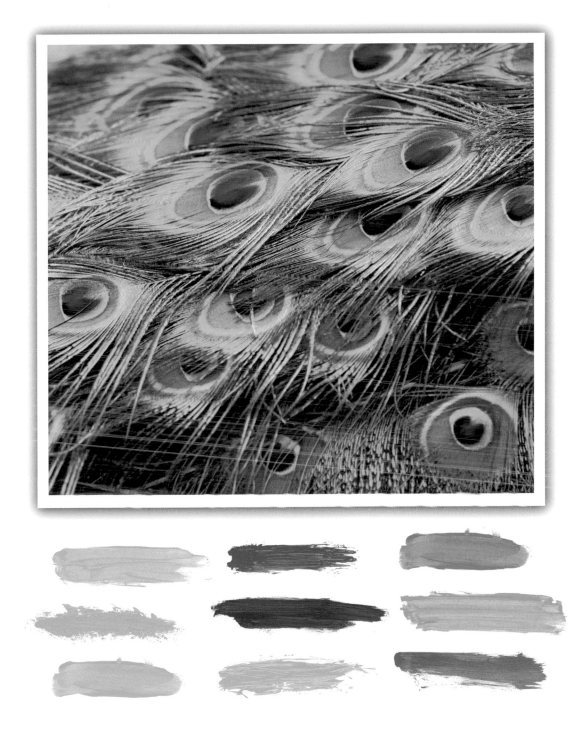

COLORFUL TRIVIA

Throughout history, turquoise has been believed to be a holy stone representative of the heavens. The domes of palaces and places of worship were covered in turquoise by the early Persians.

Native American tribes made ceremonial masks adorned in turquoise because the stone was regarded to have sacred powers. It continues to be used in religious traditions because of their belief in its protection from negative energy.

The first blue Ford Mustang was introduced in its first year of production in 1964, and Tropical Turquoise and Twilight Turquoise were two of the five blue paint shades debuted.

Blue and green are regarded as the same color in the Japanese culture. Japanese traffic lights are red, yellow, and turquoise blue, instead of the green used in America.

Turquoise is the gemstone gift given to celebrate the fifth- and eleventh-year anniversaries.

" I DARE YOU NOT TO FALL IN LOVE WITH TURQUOISE.

MOLL ANDERSON

#REVIVING TURQUOISE

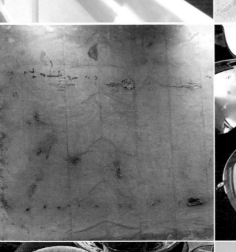

HAPPINESS
IS A CHOICE,
NOT A RESULT.
NOTHING WILL MAKE YOU HAPPY
UNTIL **CHOOSE**
YOU
TO BE HAPPY.
NO PERSON WILL MAKE YOU HAPPY
UNLESS **DECIDE**
YOU
TO BE HAPPY.
YOUR HAPPINESS WILL NOT COME TO YOU,
IT CAN ONLY COME
FROM YOU.
—Ralph Marston

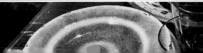

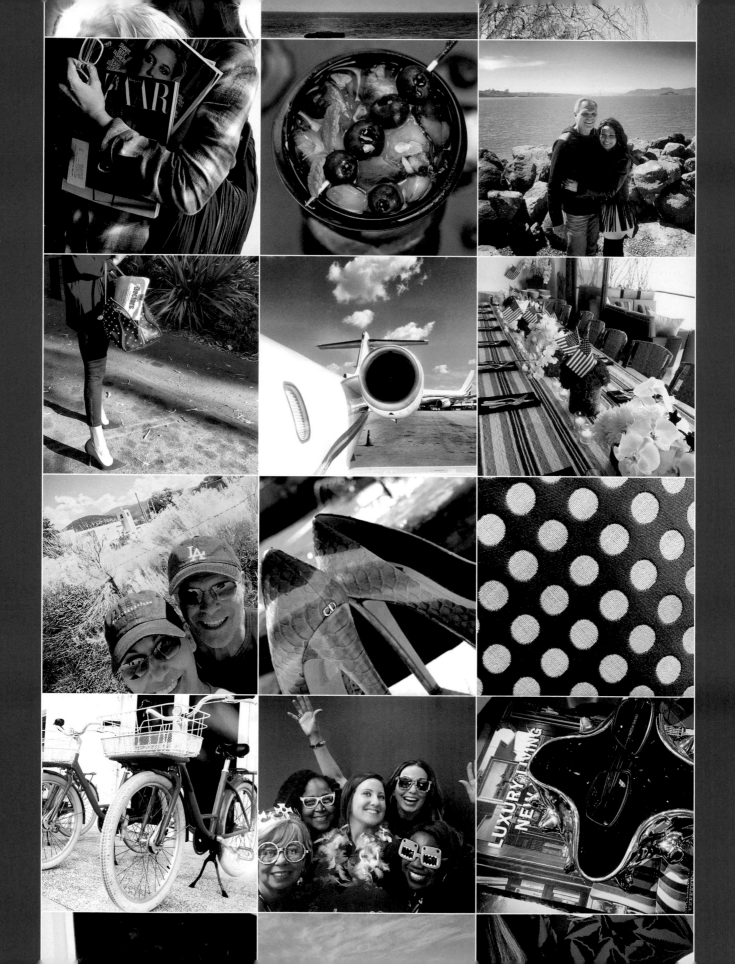

#COMFORTING BLUE

One of the primary colors, comforting blue is also one of the spectrum's most versatile colors. In relation to the elements of nature, blue elicits the calm of a clear blue sky and the powerful strength of the ocean waters. Whether bold, energetic, or peaceful, the mood you set will depend on the shade you choose. If you wish to create a soothing, relaxing vibe in your space, choose the lighter tones of sky blue, robin's egg blue, slate blue, and periwinkle. If you're craving a bold spark of energy, infuse sapphire, cobalt, and royal blue into your home décor. The classic combination of blue and white has stood the test of time, but the diverse shades, tones, and tints of blue also work in harmony with almost any color.

A universal favorite among both men and women, blue is a popular choice in home design. It represents strength, confidence, and dependability, and evokes feelings of peace, tranquility, and freshness.

moll's thought

My father had beautiful, piercing blue eyes. My husband, Charlie, has incredible bright blue eyes as well. Though I never thought to bring blue into my life until recently, I loved buying Charlie blue clothing. Seeing how he came alive in that color made me start considering blue as a possibility for our home. And now I gravitate toward cobalt and midnight blue in my own wardrobe as well.

FEELIN' KIND OF BLUE?

FLOWER *power*

One of the few true blue flowers, delphinium's name comes from the Latin word meaning dolphin due to the color and shape of the plant's bud. These hardy flowers will last approximately six to eight days in a vase, making them a perfect addition to your space. Delphinium's tall blooms make quite the statement in floral arrangements. Try letting these flowers stand high from the center of an arrangement with more compact blooms around the base, or go with only a single stem sticking out of a vase for a dramatic effect.

#POP
OF COLOR

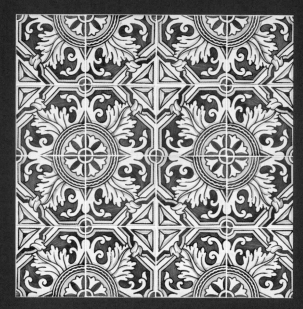

#PORCELAIN TILE

Blue and white is a classic color combination that never goes out of style. Whether it's Spanish, Italian, or Mediterranean, these tile styles are making their debuts to new generations with a modern twist. Clean and crisp and always packing a vivid vibe, this look is perfect for a kitchen, bathroom, or swimming pool. Porcelain tile in any array of colors always makes a beautiful statement. However, if porcelain is too pricey or the variation in color and uniqueness doesn't lend itself to your design aesthetics, you may want to opt for a ceramic tile. Speak to a home improvement and tile expert about durability, replacement ability, and styles when choosing the tile that will work best in your space.

#COOKWARE

Remember the colorful variety of cookware available in our play kitchens as kids? Plastic dishes, pots, and pans came in a rainbow of colors. I loved playing house with them then, and I really love playing house now. Which is why I'm so excited that color is finding its way back into grown-up kitchens by making cookware stand out in lots of gorgeous hues. Dutch ovens are a classic cookware staple that now come in so many colors to choose from, making it possible to go straight from the oven to the table with a look that is pulled together yet fun. With such vibrant colors, this cookware can double as decorative when displayed on open shelves or from a hanging rack. There are so many ways to introduce pops of color to your kitchen space. From appliances that can be special-ordered in whatever color you like to a rainbow of choices for stackable bowls and pans, kitchens have never been more exciting.

COLORFUL COCKTAIL

BLUEBERRY ELDERFLOWER GIN & TONIC

2	limes
2 ounces	gin
	Fever Tree Elderflower Tonic Water (alternatively, use 1 ounce St. Germaine and regular tonic water)
1/2 cup	fresh blueberries

Combine juice from 1 lime with gin and 2 ice cubes in a cocktail shaker and shake until chilled thoroughly. Pour gin and lime juice into a glass and top off with elderflower tonic water. Garnish with blueberries and a slice of lime.

#COLOR
LESSON

For a look that is playful and eclectic, experiment with pillows using several colors.

For a simple, sophisticated look, use blue on blue with only two pillows. To continue the monochromatic feel, add a blue throw in the same tone.

If you're like me and still crave a bit of fun, opt for a hot color for your throws, such as this yellow, which softens and brightens the feel of the room at the same time.

If balance and symmetry are important to you, arrange two or four large pillows on either side of your sofa—mixing colors that either complement or contrast with your sofa color.

The great thing about color is that it makes an impact, whether it's a little pop or multiple hues in abundance. The choice is yours—and it's easy to achieve.

This sofa was actually a neutral beige tone before Charlie and I covered it with new fabric. Although it looked great with the painting, by choosing an intense yet sophisticated blue, we were able to really electrify the room.

IN A COLORFUL ROOM, USING A METALLIC IS PERFECT FOR ACCENT CHAIRS. THE REFLECTIVE QUALITY DOESN'T FEEL LIKE YOU'RE BRINGING ANOTHER COLOR INTO THE ROOM, EVEN THOUGH YOU ARE!

#COLORSTORY

Travel opens up a brand-new world of inspiration!

On my very first trip to Europe, I was 27 years old and had no idea just how amazing the experience would be. I was awestruck as I experienced Rome, Italy—visiting the Sistine Chapel, walking through the house of Michelangelo, roaming roads where Christ actually walked, and seeing the Coliseum where so many died was emotional and life changing. The colors, the architecture, and the food were incredible. Everything I saw was an "aha moment." Several years ago I returned to Italy with my husband just for pure pleasure; until then I had only been there for work. This time I saw things in a whole new way. I took pictures of everything that affected me, from cathedrals to countrysides, from food and flowers to runways and nightlife from architecture and design to tiles and paintings on the walls. I was inspired to infuse my life with the flavor of my travels. When I returned home I discovered that the way I arranged food on a plate and flowers in a vase were more stylized. The way I dressed was even more European.

I encourage you to study your own travel pictures and explore what inspires you! Bring the colors and lifestyles of the world to you, your family, and your home.

CREATIVE FIX

Sometimes with small spaces you may want to add a little excitement to your room by using wallpaper or more than one color of paint. Why not? This is a perfect way to mix pattern play with the simplicity of white on white with blue. Remember that design, like art, is subjective. Consider what you love. The sky's the limit when you're creating your space!

COLORFUL TRIVIA

Blue is the most popular color choice for toothbrushes and is consistently ranked the most popular color in general across the world.

Mosquitoes are attracted to the color blue twice as much as they are to other colors.

Dark blue is the most common business suit color worn by world leaders—reported to be the top color choice for job interviews.

The largest animal ever known to have existed is the blue whale, at nearly 390,000 pounds.

The sky is blue because molecules in the Earth's atmosphere scatter blue light from the sun more than other colors because blue light travels in shorter wavelengths.

The original ultramarine pigment used by Renaissance painters was made by grinding lapis lazuli into powder. It was the finest and most expensive blue.

" WE ALL HAVE ONE IDEA OF WHAT THE COLOR BLUE IS, BUT PRESSED TO DESCRIBE IT SPECIFICALLY, THERE ARE SO MANY WAYS: THE OCEAN, LAPIS LAZULI, THE SKY, SOMEONE'S EYES. OUR DEFINITIONS ARE AS DIFFERENT AS WE ARE OURSELVES.

SARAH DESSEN

#COMFORTING BLUE

I WANT TO MEET
SOMEONE THAT
MAKES ME FEEL THE
WAY MUSIC DOES.
—unknown

#ENRICHING VIOLET

molli's thought

Violet has been calling to me this year! It started with some anemones that I purchased in amazing hues of purple and violet. They sparked a thrill that went from my head down to my toes, and I knew I had to have them. My spiritual side was craving the healing tones of violet, which then motivated me to take a giant leap and add this elegant color to several walls with a beautiful Venetian plaster. I smile every time I walk by!

Purple, commonly known as the color of royalty, is a mix of empowering, life-sustaining red and heavenly blue, and elicits a range of emotions. The bluer cool purples lend a feeling of tranquility, while the redder hues are emotionally hotter and more dramatic. Variations in the color purple encompass the entire spectrum and include the bright hues of violet and blue-violet, true purple, and grape, the deeper shades of aubergine and plum, and the lighter pastel tints of lilac and lavender. No matter which shade you prefer, purple has the power to set the mood of your space.

Recently emerging as a modern design choice for the home, purple is sophisticated, elegant, playful, romantic, and funky. Regardless of the shade you choose, it will change your home's vibe in a positive way.

The healing powers found in the purple amethyst is said to offer spiritual growth and protection. Purple represents everything from spirituality, creativity, and romance to wealth, pride, and elegance.

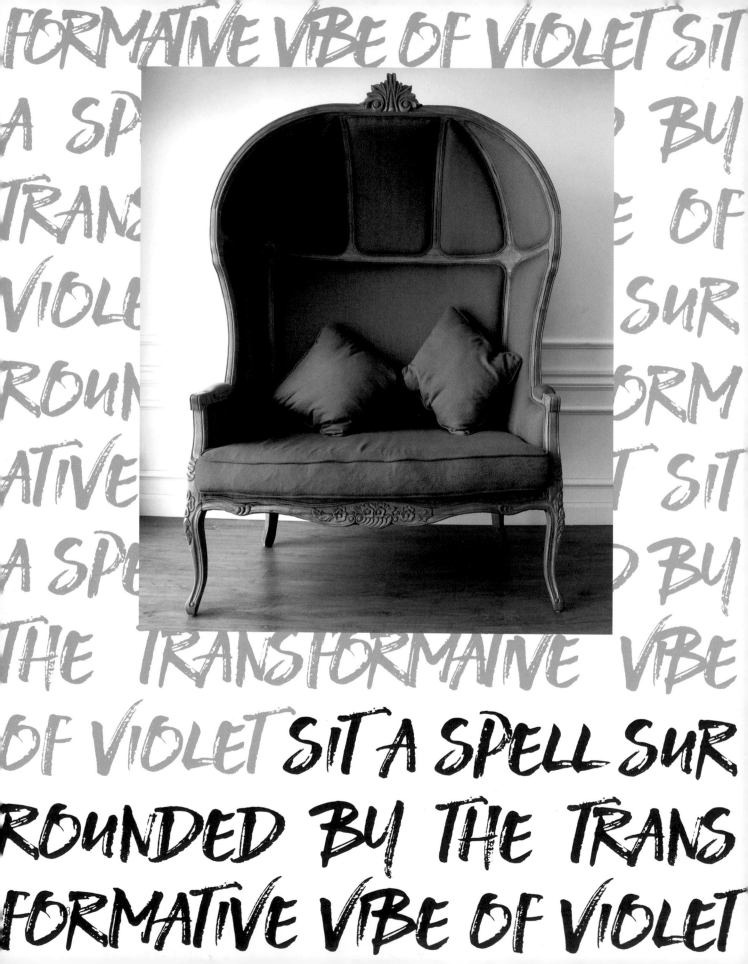

SIT A SPELL SUR
ROUNDED BY THE TRANS
FORMATIVE VIBE OF VIOLET

FLOWER *power*

Exotic and modern, orchids pack a premium punch with their long-lasting blooms in impressive shapes and colors. These tropical plants have no cold tolerance, don't require a lot of attention, and have blooms that last 4 to 6 weeks or more, making them popular houseplants. To easily water them, place a few ice cubes at the base of each plant once a week. An orchid plant is the perfect accent to a powder room or bedside table, or combine several plants in a container and cover with moss for a larger, eye-catching arrangement. A single bloom is a simple, and oh-so-special touch to a place setting, and unsprayed orchids are a gorgeous garnish for food and beverages when all you need is a little flower power.

#POP
OF COLOR

#DINING CHAIRS

As many homeowners knock down walls to create more open spaces, dining rooms are now becoming part of the overall living space. Even if you didn't originally have a dining area, you can define a space for one by floating your dining table and chairs in your living space.

Dining chairs can be an expensive purchase, especially if you desire a well-made chair. However, they can be the perfect way to easily and affordably add color to your space. If you're on a budget, consider purchasing a simple dining table and splurging on the chairs, which don't need to match. Just be sure your chair height fits with the table you're using. Fortunately, well-made chairs can be both comfortable and beautiful. Introduce color to the space by buying bright, colorful chairs or by adding slipcovers.

#NECKTIES

Until recently, neckties were the only way men had to pop some color into their wardrobes, and it's still a great way to express their mood du jour and showcase a flair for style. While recent novels have put the spotlight back on neckwear, skyrocketing the sales of gray neckties, purple ties in all shades have been climbing the sales charts as well. Violet's full spectrum of hues really works well in men's suiting—from sophisticated and regal to playful and fun loving.

But where in the world did neckties originate, and why?

In the seventeenth century, around the Thirty Years' War in France, it is said that King Louis XIII hired Croatian mercenaries who wore uniforms that had a colorful cloth around their necks. Although the reason for the cloth was functional—it tied the top of their jackets—the king loved them so much that he ordered them to be worn to all royal events.

COLORFUL COCKTAIL

LAVENDER LEMON DROP

¹/₂ cup	sugar
¹/₂ cup	water
1 tablespoon	lavender buds
¹/₄ cup	Stoli Vanil™ vodka
1	lemon, cut in wedges
	Club soda or sparkling water

Make lavender simple syrup by bringing sugar, water, and lavender to a boil. Turn off heat, strain the lavender buds, and chill completely. In a shaker, combine the vodka, squeeze of a lemon wedge, 1 tablespoon simple syrup, and ice; shake to chill. Pour into a glass and top with a splash of club soda or sparkling water.

CREATIVE FIX

Paying attention to details is something I encourage my clients and readers to do. It's the difference between a well-designed space and one that seems not quite finished, like something is missing. It's the exclamation point to BAM! With the right color and accessories, this billiard table looks like it's begging you to shoot a game.

Accessorizing is not too difficult, especially when it's all about bringing color into your space. The purple felt on the pool table makes this beautiful violet bottle come to life, and the purple tulips are a huge bang for the buck. Candles and trays are an easy way to create a well-appointed room, even when it's just a place for family to gather. The design choices you make create your lifestyle.

Anyone who knows me expects to see a dressing table in any home I create. Even during times when I worked with a smaller budget, I found a way to make a dressing table. I believe that every woman needs a place to sit and breathe, listen to music, and prepare for the day. Your dressing table should be designed in a way that reflects what's beautiful to you. You should feel special in that chair.

The vibe for my Dallas dressing table is delectable, daring, Art Deco, and all about color! This amazing painting infuses energy into my mornings, and I chose the violet from the painting for my vase, throw, and flowers, which pulled it all together.

When hanging a painting above your dressing table or above any table, don't be afraid of extending beyond the lines of the furniture. The effect can be exciting.

Any framed mirror can have a stand added to the back to enble it to sit on your table.

FOR EUROPEAN DRAMA, HANG A LARGE, GILDED, FRAMED MIRROR ON THE WALL, PAINT A SIMPLE TABLE, COVER THE TOP WITH GLASS, AND ADD A VELVET-CUSHIONED BENCH.

#COLORSTORY

Sometimes you need to live in a space before you can really understand how you and your family will use it.

This space, which housed our pool table, proved to be the perfect space to double as our formal dining area. After pondering how could I use this space two different ways, it became clear to me that the wall behind the bar wasn't warm and inviting enough for dining and felt more like an open pantry. We removed the shelves and penny-sized tiles and plastered to match the rest of the space. We found a painting that filled the space exactly, within 2 inches all around, and with the perfect shades to create a more sophisticated vibe. By choosing a hue between the violet and flesh-tone pink colors in the painting we took our barstools to another level in a sparkling metallic fabric.

Purple was the first man-made color dye and was prized due to its beauty and scarcity.

Throughout history, the color purple has been associated with royalty and worn by emperors, kings, nobles, and priests.

Carrots were originally purple, with the occasional mutated version occurring in shades of orange, yellow, and white, before sixteenth-century Dutch growers gradually developed them into the orange variety of today.

Of all the primary and secondary colors, violet/purple is the least occurring in nature, leading to its association with the artificial and unconventional.

The flag of Dominica, an island in the Caribbean, is the only national flag in the world to include the color violet or purple.

Louisiana, Texas, and West Virginia all have cities named Violet.

> **ALL THE OTHER COLORS ARE JUST COLORS, BUT PURPLE SEEMS TO HAVE A SOUL —WHEN YOU LOOK AT IT, IT'S LOOKING BACK AT YOU.**

UNIEK SWAIN

#ENRICHING VIOLET

I ASPIRE TO INSPIRE

BEFORE I EXPIRE

—Eugene Bell, Jr.

IF YOU COULD TAKE A SELFIE OF YOUR SOUL WOULD YOU FIND IT ATTRACTIVE ENOUGH TO POST?
-unknown

#UPLIFTING PINK

Romantic, whimsical, fun, and flirty, the many shades of uplifting pink are filled with personality. The color of love, pink is a combination of red and white—red being fiery hot and passionate, while pink is more romantic and charming. The brighter pinks of fuchsia, hot pink, shocking pink, and magenta have more red, making them bolder as they assert a vibrant and powerful energy. The softer pastel pinks of blush, rose quartz, dusty rose, and mauve are more subdued and sophisticated.

Pink can be paired with a variety of colors including whites and neutrals, chocolate brown, black, gray, and navy. When designing with masculine colors like black and gray, pink adds a feminine balance. It also creates a rosy glow in your space that provides a healthy atmosphere. Pink has the power to soothe the heart and fill it with joy, peace, love, playfulness, and tenderness.

moll's thought

What is it about pink that immediately makes you think of little girls and frilly dresses? I used to be so out of touch with my feminine side that I tended to avoid pink completely. Not anymore! Now I love that girly side of me, wearing and designing with pink whenever I get the chance. And I love that men are now embracing this hue as well! Everywhere you turn in menswear pink is being showcased—from pink socks and ties to sweaters, and dress shirts.

FLOWER *power*

"Roses as big as cabbages," is how peonies were described by explorer Marco Polo upon first glance, and it's no surprise these stunning, timeless blooms have been prized by flower lovers ever since. Packed full of papery, delicate petals, peonies are best bought with the buds still balled up so you can enjoy the blooming process. Peonies are available around the end of April, with their season lasting as late as the beginning of July. Cabbage roses, English garden roses, and dahlias mix beautifully with peonies, as well as serving as similar alternatives outside of peony season.

#POP OF COLOR

#SHOES

Be still, my heart! There's nothing like a pair of shoes to get you excited—and when they're in hot, haute pink, there's not much to do other than give a shout out to the girl who's fabulous enough to wear them!

There's nothing that declares your style like a pair of shoes in any pop of color. Even if you love living in your basic black outfits, adding a colorful pair of shoes will pump up the volume of your wardrobe and especially your day. Be daring and try it—see what happens when others feast their eyes on your colorful stilettos or kicks. Not sure how to choose? Visit your favorite footwear department and see which color jumps out and says, "Take me home." Let the shoes choose you.

#BLUSH

Regardless of skin tone, everyone looks better with a healthy pink glow. Years ago, women would pinch their cheeks to bring a bit of color to their faces in order to look healthy and pretty. Where did this idea originate? When we blush, the blood rushes to our cheeks, giving us an appearance of liveliness and possibly being in love. We often try to replicate this sun-kissed look by spending time outside. Today, thanks to all the fabulous makeup companies, there is no end to the choices of pink hues and tints to bring some color back to our skin after long, hard days of work and travel. I never go anywhere without my blush in my purse. From soft pink to bronzing sunset tones, there's a color that's perfect for you to put some pizzazz into your cheeks and give you a radiant glow.

COLORFUL COCKTAIL

RHUBARB ROSE

2 stalks	rhubarb, chopped
1/4 cup	water
1/2 teaspoon	rose water
1 ounce	vodka
1 ounce	St. Germaine
1 teaspoon	freshly squeezed lemon juice

Bring the rhubarb and water to a boil in a small saucepan. Let cook for 15 minutes until the rhubarb is tender. Strain the cooked rhubarb and chill the liquid thoroughly. Combine the strained and chilled rhubarb juice with the rose water, vodka, St. Germaine, lemon juice, and 3 ice cubes in a cocktail shaker. Shake the mixture well until the drink is thoroughly chilled, and serve.

This bright tone of pink, when mixed with slate gray, was a strong but risky color combo for the terrace. The idea of a huge pink sofa was scary; however, the thought of playing it safe was much more uncomfortable for me at that time in my life. I really wanted to trust my color instincts and my desire to create a new vibe with this color. And I'm so glad I did! I love this space and the reactions people have when they see this sofa. Even if they have an aversion to pink, it still elicits a reaction from them, and often the response is, "I wish I had the guts to have a wild-colored sofa."

When using a fun, bold pop of color like fuchsia, especially on a large statement piece, balance it with neutrals on the rest of your furniture and accessories.

Dark painted or lacquered wood adds a powerful statement for your coffee table and accessories.

Use vinyl for outdoor living, which is so durable, especially when you live in places with varying weather conditions. It also comes in many amazing colors to add that zest to any space, inside or out.

When planning your outdoor living space, use the same design sense as you would on your indoor spaces. Include all the essentials for creating a cozy, relaxing, sensory-scaped living space outdoors.

CANVAS COVERS FOR OUTDOOR FURNITURE ARE A MUST TO PROTECT FURNITURE FROM WEATHER AND SUN DAMAGE. STORE PILLOWS IN AN OUTDOOR CABINET OR KEEP THEM INSIDE.

#COLORSTORY

There is something magical about the holidays. We all have color stories relating to our childhood experiences, whether you celebrated Christmas with red and green or Hanukkah with blue and silver. These memories certainly affect how you choose to celebrate today. Traditions that are carried on often evolve from the happy times your family had together, while negative memories may force certain traditions to be discontinued. When I became in charge of my own family's holiday traditions, I longed to decorate an amazing tree in traditional Christmas colors.

But life happens, and during financially difficult times and particularly after water filled my basement one year, destroying all my ornaments, I learned to design on a dime. I found long strands of plastic ivy and grape bunches for 80 percent off and spray-painted them metallic gold. Even after I got back on my feet, I knew that I would continue to create fantasy trees for my grandchildren. Regardless of my budget, I could contribute to their very own positive color stories about Christmas!

COLORFUL TRIVIA

Pink is one of the favorite colors in India, symbolizing love, and is associated with the Indian spiritual leader Meher Baba.

In the 1950s, Madame Ritz of the Ritz Hotel in Paris requested that all lampshades be lined in pink because of the flattering light it illuminated.

Studies have shown that women weightlifters tend to show increased strength around the color pink, whereas males seem to have a decreased level of strength in rooms of this color.

Lake Hillier, located on the largest island in Australia, is a lake in which the water is a permanent color of pink and does not change even when put into a container.

Margarine was dyed pink in the 1880s to mark the difference between butter substitutes and real butter.

Members of the Dianthus family, flowers called pinks are where the color pink got its name.

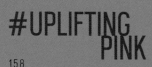

#UPLIFTING PINK

158

"PINK ISN'T JUST A COLOR, IT'S AN ATTITUDE!

MILEY CYRUS

EVERYTIME I DANCE, I TURN INTO A BETTER VERSION OF ME

#EMPOWERING RED

The color of love, life, passion, and danger, empowering red demands your attention. This fiery color heightens the senses and stimulates an emotional and physical response—elevating the heart rate, increasing blood flow, and boosting energy. In your home, a touch of red adds excitement, energy, and warmth to your space. Regardless of the design style, red is a popular choice for creating mood, with plenty of shades to choose from—orangey reds like poppy; purple and brown shades such as marsala and burgundy; the vibrant, hot reds of scarlet, ruby, and crimson; and fire engine red, for those ready to turn up the heat. Not a color to be hidden inside, red makes a welcoming statement on the exterior of your home as well—think doors and shutters.

The longest wavelength of color, red excites the strongest emotions in every culture. Filled with meaning, red evokes conflicting emotions—anger and love, life and death, excitement and danger.

moll's thought

Have you ever noticed when a woman walks into a room wearing a red dress everyone turns to look? Some people may think it's too daring, but I love it when a woman is confident enough to wear red. I once hosted a red party and presented the option of wearing red or black. I was amazed at how many women chose to wear black even when encouraged with the opportunity to go red!

161

FLOWER *power*

Fragrant and timeless, roses have long held an allure as they speak of passion and romance. Their many colors are readily available almost anywhere, from the hometown grocery store to the city street corner. When working with fresh-cut roses, remove any outer petals that are discolored or weathered and leaves that would be below water level in the vase. For bigger blooms, blow in the center of the flower to loosen it and gently bend back the outer petals one at a time. These romantic flowers instantly create a colorful vibe in any space.

#POP
OF COLOR

#DRESSER

For years, dressers have been available in the traditional wood tones, but I'm so excited that now so many are painting, staining, and lacquering dressers and other furniture in great colors that can perk up a tired room. Not only are the color possibilities endless, there are plenty of finishes to choose from as well! From glamorous high gloss to subtle matte, these finishes can transform an ordinary piece of furniture into an eye-catching statement piece.

What better way to command attention than with the energy of empowering red! Introduce this color with a standout dresser or set of fab lamps to add life to your space.

#LIPSTICK

Nothing packs a powerful punch of color to your smile like bold, red lips. Although finding the right shade takes a little bit of practice, once you discover your color, you can wear it confidently. First, identify your skin tone to reveal what will work with your complexion. While a color may look fabulous on a friend, it may not work as well with your skin tone. The veins on your wrists are key to this discovery: If they're mostly blue and purple, you have a cool undertone; if they are mostly green, you have a warm undertone; a mix of both indicates a neutral undertone. Those with cool undertones (pale, porcelain skin) should opt for a lipstick with a blue base. If you have warm undertones (olive or yellowy complexions), go for orangey-red shades; those with darker skin can try either or choose a pink-based red, which could look spectacular.

COLORFUL COCKTAIL

HIBISCUS, LEMON, & BASIL COOLER

10	dried hibiscus flowers
$^1/_2$ cup	water
$^1/_2$ cup	granulated sugar
4	fresh basil leaves, plus more for garnish
2 ounces	fresh lemon juice, plus peel for garnish
2 ounces	vodka

Make hibiscus simple syrup by combining the dried hibiscus flowers, water, and sugar in a small saucepan and bring to a boil. Turn off the heat and let sit for 15 minutes. Strain the syrup and chill thoroughly. Muddle basil in the bottom of a cocktail shaker and combine $^1/_2$ cup of the hibiscus simple syrup, the lemon juice, and vodka. Shake well with two ice cubes. Pour the hibiscus mixture over ice into two cocktail glasses. Garnish with fresh basil and a lemon peel.

#COLOR
LESSON

your neighborhood is conservative, your front door can be your self-expression piece.

Red is one of the most popular door colors, and adds a bit of personality and contrast to the front of your home.

When choosing a shade of red for your door, visit a paint store and consider which shade you gravitate toward and what makes you feel happy.

After choosing several samples, paint them directly on your door a few inches apart. Consider how the color brightens or deepens once it has dried, and during different times of day, to get the true color effect.

Your front door is one of the first things people see when they visit your home. What does it say to the world? Although we spend most of our time inside our houses, the outside of our homes should reflect our style as well! While it's important to have a sturdy, practical entrance, you don't have to sacrifice style. Make your door a welcoming statement piece with color. Don't be afraid to go bold, especially if you have a neutral exterior. Even if

THE CHINESE CULTURE BELIEVES RED TO BE A LUCKY COLOR. PAINTING YOUR FRONT DOOR RED IS RECOMMENDED IN FENG SHUI TO INVITE PROSPERITY TO ALL WHO LIVE INSIDE THE HOUSE.

#COLORSTORY

I often meet people who are afraid to jump straight into a power color for their home. This is when I suggest that they start with their wardrobe. A pair of boots, a purse, or a fabulous fall coat may be just the solution! If that's still too much color, how about an inexpensive umbrella? It's definitely a fun pop of color—and it will be easy to find among all the black umbrellas at coat check on a rainy day.

The idea is to bring some color and excitement to your life in a simple way by starting small and seeing how it makes you feel when you wear it. I feel a rush of excitement every time I find something red to wear. Although it's a perfect choice for romance, it's also a perfect pick for a job interview—let them know that you are confident and ready to take on a new position!

It is believed babies see red as their first color once their eyes mature beyond the initial visual recognition of contrasting black and white.

At twilight, red is the first color you lose sight of.

Bees can see all bright colors except red; therefore, red flowers are usually pollinated by other means.

For people with red hair, it generally takes up to 20 percent more anesthesia to be put under compared to people with other hair colors.

Red symbolizes joy, fortune, good luck, and protection in many Asian cultures and is a widely used color. Being seen as a color of happiness, in the Chinese culture, red is strictly prohibited at funerals.

Scarlet is an orange-red worn by the cardinals of the Roman Catholic Church, and because of its coloring that is how the cardinal bird got its name.

"RED IS SUCH AN INTERESTING COLOR TO CORRELATE WITH EMOTION, BECAUSE IT'S ON BOTH ENDS OF THE SPECTRUM. ON ONE END YOU HAVE HAPPINESS, FALLING IN LOVE, INFATUATION WITH SOMEONE, PASSION, ALL THAT. ON THE OTHER END, YOU'VE GOT OBSESSION, JEALOUSY, DANGER, FEAR, ANGER AND FRUSTRATION.

TAYLOR SWIFT

#EMPOWERING RED

CONFIDENCE
IS THE
SEXIEST
THING A WOMAN CAN HAVE
IT'S MUCH SEXIER
THAN ANY BODY PART.
—Aimee Mullins

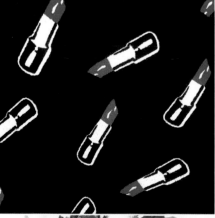

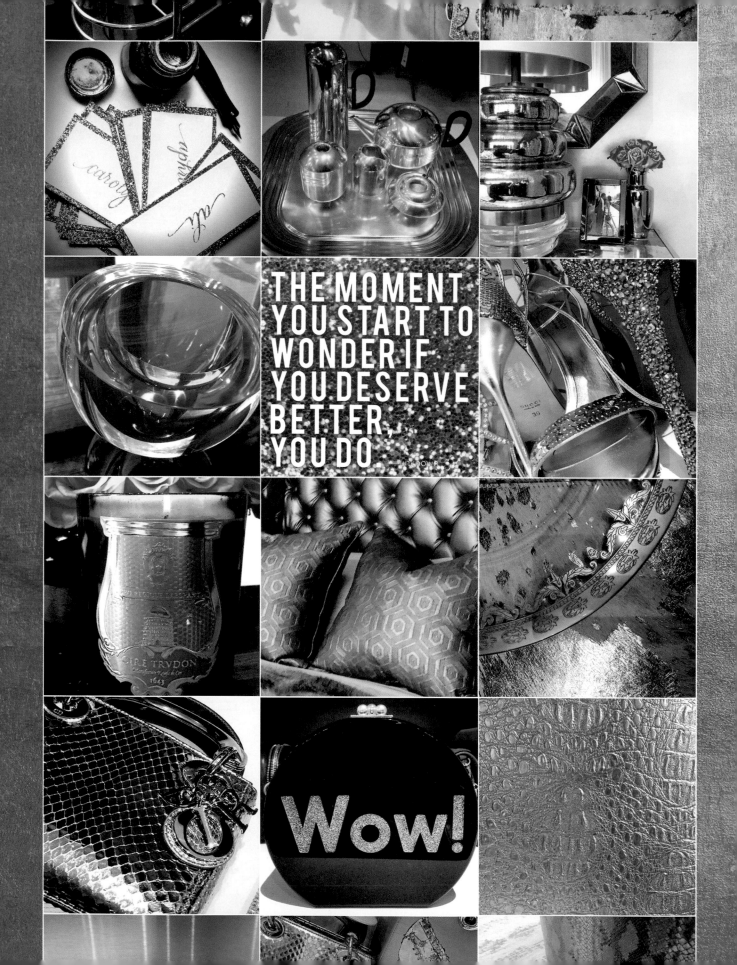

THE MOMENT YOU START TO WONDER IF YOU DESERVE BETTER, YOU DO

Wow!

#MOTIVATING METALS

Bring on the shine! A shimmering touch of motivating metals will make a powerful impact in your home. From polished and shining to brushed and matte finishes, metal elements add a timeless elegance and a bit of "glam" to your home. Gold, brass and bronze, silver, chrome, nickel, copper, and iron, metals mix well with any decorating styles. Metallic finishes bring a textural element to your home and work with almost any color palette.

Adorn a ceiling with gold leaf or add metallic in your wall coverings and fabrics. But the best, easiest way to introduce metals in your space is with your furnishings and accessories. Chairs, vases, nightstands, mirrors, fabrics, fixtures, lighting, and accent pieces—a touch of motivating metal can light the way to wow. Gold, a warm, masculine color associated with the sun, represents quality, elegance, wealth, and prestige. Silver is a cool precious metal that also represents wealth and prestige but is considered a feminine color associated with the moon.

moll's thought

It's always interesting to watch how certain trends come back around. But in my heart, metallic has never gone out of style. Oh, how I love sparkle and shine. I'm loving that more homes have now invited metallics to move right in and make themselves comfortable in places you might not expect—everything from a simple touch of metal to some serious glamour to your lifestyle!

FLOWER *power*

#POP
OF COLOR

#LIGHTING

Think of lighting, such as chandeliers and sconces, as jewelry for your home. They frame your space in the same way earrings frame your face. There are so many fabulous ways to light your home, and the reflective nature of metals adds an amazing effect to the ambiance of your home. If you're not sure which color of metallics to choose, look at your jewelry; it will reveal which metals you typically gravitate toward.

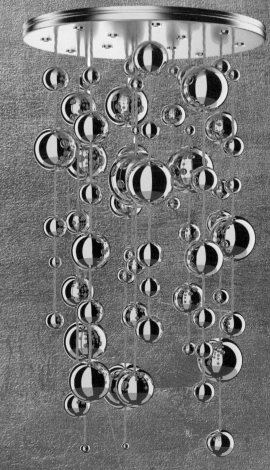

Succulents can thrive with limited water sources, making them lower maintenance than most indoor plants. The various textures and natural green color create a contemporary and organic look. The smooth, waxy leaves offer the option to have a little fun. Although I prefer fresh flowers, because there's nothing like the real thing, succulents are great if you would like to go the no-maintenance route; try the fabulous-looking faux option—you can hardly tell the difference. Succulents sit pretty atop a simple bed of rocks or moss, and they are the perfect addition to flower arrangements or potted plants. Add a touch of modern metal to a cool container by spray painting the succulent with a high-shine metallic paint. You can even increase the reflective factor by adding glitter for holidays or parties.

#MOSAIC TILE

Mosaics, which are designs created from small pieces of tile or stone, are widely popular in decorating, and have been around for thousands of years. From the earthy, natural effect to the sleek, polished feel, mosaics are incredibly versatile. Metallics in tiles have become the new staple for the home and will remain just as timeless, taking something traditional to a whole new design level. With so many choices, it's important to seek advice from a professional. Some tiles are very fragile, while others are quite durable. Mosaic tiles are a great way to achieve an expensive look on a budget. While mosaics may create a particular image, a pattern or random arrangement is a popular option. If going fully metallic scares you, then opt for a combination of neutral, earthy tiles with an accent of metallics for a more low-key shine—even a little sparkle goes a long way.

GRILLED PINEAPPLE MULE

1/2	fresh pineapple, cored and sliced into 2-inch pieces lengthwise
2	limes, juiced
10	fresh mint leaves
4 ounces	vodka
	Fever Tree Ginger Beer

Heat grill to medium-high heat. Place the pineapple slices onto the grill and cook for 2 minutes per side until the pineapple has grill marks but isn't cooked through. Let pineapple cool completely; then chop. Combine 1/2 cup of the grilled pineapple, juice from the limes, mint leaves, and vodka in a cocktail shaker. Muddle the pineapple and mint leaves until all of the flavors have been released. Shake well and pour over ice. Top off the cocktail with ginger beer and serve immediately. Makes enough to for 2 short mule mugs.

Every master bedroom or guest room needs a teacart or bar cart. It's a Moll Must-Have, even in the smallest spaces! In a master bedroom, a cart is a great way to provide a mini escape for parents before the day begins or after the kids are in bed at the end of a long day. It's also a great addition to a guest room. Offer guests their favorite beverage and a snack of fruit, cheese and crackers, or nuts as a welcoming treat. It creates a wonderful surprise and allows them to quietly rest and relax after a day of travel. Don't forget to include some fresh flowers and a candle with the signature scent of your home.

Carts are very popular these days, making them easy to find. Whether you need something extra small or extra fabulous, finding the right size is an adventure. Antique stores are the perfect place to discover wonderfully cool carts.

A cart is also a great piece when you need a little extra serving space. It can be rolled or moved inside or outside and it can double as a bar or a place for guests to set drinks while mingling.

A decorative metal box placed on the cart works perfectly in guest rooms to store first-aid items, pain relievers, schedules, helpful information for your guests, and your WI-FI password.

EARLY NINETEENTH-CENTURY TEACARTS WERE ALSO REFERRED TO AS TEA TROLLEYS. THESE WERE OFTEN USED TO PRESENT AND IMPRESS GUESTS WITH FINGER SANDWICHES AND REFRESHMENTS, BUT MOST IMPORTANT, TO SHOW OFF THE HOSTESS'S FINE TEA SET.

#COLORSTORY

I love the before-and-after segments on television for a home that needs a bit of attention! When you take a piece of furniture and completely transform it from drab to fab, it's so exciting! There's such satisfaction in creating that transformation. This taupe leather chair was a beautiful design, but the combination of color and style did not do the chair any favors. It was very plain and looked like it was made to blend in rather than stand out.

When I inherited two of these chairs, I loved that they were super comfy, but they lacked luster, to say the least. Because we had already chosen so much color for our art and in our sofa and accessories, I really wanted these chairs to have their shining moment in our space. Edelman has a wonderful selection of metallic leathers, and I knew when I saw this glistening silver leather that this would be the burst of wow the room needed. It wouldn't compete in the space; it would simply reflect the light and be the icing on the cake.

EDELMAN®

COLORFUL TRIVIA

Silver reigned as the most popular color for new cars from 2001 to 2006.

In 1934, one of Germany's racecars was just slightly overweight, so all of the paint was removed, leaving the silver body visible. After the car won the race, they adopted silver as their racing color.

Copper is believed to have been used for over 10,000 years. It is 100 percent recyclable and retains 95 percent of its original value, allowing the majority of copper that we have produced to remain in use.

The word *silver* is one of the few words in the English language that is nearly impossible to rhyme.

Copper is a natural antibacterial, making it a popular metal for doorknobs and handrails, especially in public places. Silver has also been incorporated into clothing and shoes through coated yarns due to its ability to inhibit bacteria and fungi growth in clothing.

#MOTIVATING METALS

188

> " I THINK IT'S BEAUTIFUL TO BE ABLE TO COVER YOURSELF IN METAL. I LOVE THE COLOR AND THE WAY IT REFLECTS. BUT IT IS ALSO A PROTECTION.

— DAPHNE GUINNESS

#NURTURING NEUTRALS

Shades of white and cream, mixes of beige, taupe, and gray—there is no limit to the number of neutral shades. Whether it's the warm tones of beige and cream or the cooler tones of gray, taupe, and cool white, a neutral palette is the perfect backdrop for making a statement with color.

Neutrals have a timeless quality that will work with any design style, and it doesn't have to be dull and uninteresting.

With an all-neutral monochromatic color scheme, use more than one neutral shade to enhance architectural details and create depth. Include textural elements in your furnishings, fabrics, and accessories. When using neutral tones on your walls, contrast with deeper colors such as black, chocolate brown, or rich jewel tones or add accent pieces in bold pops of color. The color of golden sand, weathered stone, and the natural earth, organic neutrals are associated with freshness, tradition, tranquility, and security.

moll's thought

When I think of neutrals, my sense memories come alive. The first thing that comes to mind is our yard in Tennessee when snow has just fallen, making everything beautiful, even well-worn houses and naked trees. I remember the creamy white beaches of Destin, Florida, and the beautiful blonde hair of my sweet grandmother. I recall the smell of creamy mashed potatoes on Thanksgiving, and the taste of vanilla ice cream that Harlow, my precious Cavalier King Charles, loves to taste from Charlie's bowl.

FLOWER *power*

There's something simply stunning about a bouquet of hydrangea and the way mounds of the snowball-like blooms create a classic and elegant feel in any space. Hydrangeas work well with any color palette and can stand alone or combine with countless other blooms. Because their stems produce a "sap" that can block their ability to absorb water, there are several things to keep in mind when arranging fresh hydrangeas. You can break the stems to avoid blockage, or when cutting, smash the bottom of the cut stem with a wooden mallet, dip it in boiling water for thirty seconds immediately before adding them to a vase, or dip the end of the stem into powdered alum (found in the grocery store spice aisle) to aid water absorption in the arrangement. Hydrangeas can actually drink water through their blooms, so if they start to look limp, soak the blooms in water for 15 to 45 minutes; they will perk right back up. With a little loving care, they will stay fresh and full for one to two weeks.

#POP OF COLOR

#SOFA

Sofas are one of the biggest investments for your living space, and a neutral fabric offers a classic versatility that will last for years. A neutral sofa also offers a great backdrop for colorful pillows and accessories, which can easily and affordably be switched out to create whatever vibe you want. The traditional look of this sofa works well because the slipcover gives it a more relaxed look. It can be used with just about any style. A slipcovered sofa is a great choice, since the cover is removable, making it easier to clean, and providing the option of changing the cover later. It is extremely important to consider the size of your room when choosing a sofa. Guessing is not an option, so be sure to have room and doorway measurements handy when shopping. You don't want to fall in love with a sofa only to discover it won't fit through your door.

#FAUX FUR

Fe, Fi, Faux Fur! Don't you love the soft texture and lush vibe that faux fur brings to your home? Not only does it look great but it provides warmth to a space. With so many great European companies perfecting the look of expensive furs, you have to look pretty hard to tell the difference. From pillow covers to rugs to throws for the foot of your bed or couch, there are many options for adding faux fur to your space. Besides animal rights issues, there are many advantages of faux fur over real fur. Faux fur is more resistant to insect damage and more stable to temperature and moisture changes. Be sure to follow the cleaning directions carefully on your individual faux fur items. Although some are washable, others are dry clean only. With such comfort, curling up with a glass of wine will never be the same.

COLORFUL COCKTAIL

PEAR & THYME CHAMPAGNE

4	fresh thyme sprigs
1/2 cup	sugar
1/2 cup	water
1	ripe pear, peeled, cored
	Dry champagne

Make a thyme simple syrup by bringing the thyme sprigs, sugar, and water to a boil. Turn off the heat and chill completely. Puree the pear with 2 tablespoons of thyme simple syrup. Strain the pear and thyme purée if you desire. Place 1 tablespoon of the pear and thyme purée into the bottom of a champagne glass. Fill the rest of the glass with champagne and serve immediately.

Ottomans come in all sizes and shapes, from plush and tufted, to round and smooth, to angular and modern. Some even double as storage, and many can be used as extra seating in a pinch. Ottomans can add style, color, and an artsy element to your space, offering an option for everyone.

Ottomans are an affordable way to infuse color and pattern into your space. When added to a neutral palette, a bold ottoman can make a color statement.

A large-scaled ottoman can double as a coffee table by adding a tray to set drinks and plates. It also provides a place to put your feet up comfortably.

Examine the craftsmanship of an ottoman before you buy it to ensure that its structure is sound for setting dishes or using as extra seating.

When shopping for an ottoman, bring a tape measure to be sure it fits in your space when you bring it home.

OTTOMANS ARE A WELL-USED ITEM, SO YOUR FABRIC CHOICE IS AN IMPORTANT CONSIDERATION. IF YOU HAVE PETS AND CHILDREN, THINK ABOUT A DURABLE, STAIN-RESISTANT FABRIC OR SLIPCOVERS FOR EASY CLEANING.

#COLORSTORY

A guest bathroom is a mini showroom, so have some fun with it. Create a bathroom you would love to visit yourself. It's definitely a place your guests will see and use, so make it beautiful, well-lit, and fresh. An important element to consider when designing your guest bathroom is the lighting. To determine whether the lighting is good, try applying makeup, tweezing a brow, or shaving, if you're a guy. If it's difficult to do those tasks, change the lighting or offer a hand mirror or magnified mirror with a light to assist your guests. Good lighting and mirrors and a soft, neutral palette will provide a relaxing retreat your guests are sure to love.

The human eye can distinguish approximately 500 shades of gray.

In ancient Greek culture, people wore white to bed to bring pleasant dreams.

Brides and bridesmaids dressed in all white up until the early 1800s.

Peanut M&Ms only appeared in the color tan when they were first introduced in 1954.

White is probably the most universally used color in interior design and the typical color for ceilings, bathrooms, trim, and appliances. It is commonly found in modern interiors to highlight architecture as the main focus.

The color "buff" got its name from the color of un-dyed, buffed leather. During the 17th century, English soldiers wore tunics of buffed leather, coining the phrase "in the buff." Because of the perception that (English) skin is buff-colored, the phrase evolved into its modern day meaning as being naked.

#NURTURING NEUTRALS

202

"NEUTRAL TONES ARE THE PERFECT BACKDROP TO ALLOW ACCESSORIES AND ART TO BRING ON THE WOW FACTOR!

MOLL ANDERSON

"IF THE
WHOLE
WORLD WAS
BLIND,
HOW MANY
PEOPLE
WOULD YOU
IMPRESS?"
—Boonaa Mohammed

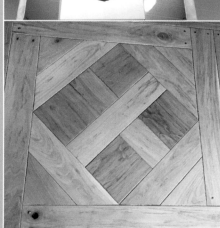

DON'T BE
ashamed of
your story
IT WILL
INSPIRE OTHERS
—unknown

SAVANNAH BEE COMPANY.

#SOFTENING PASTELS

Adding white to the rainbow of colors will create the pastel palette—pale pink, lavender, sky blue, butter yellow, pale peach, and mint green. But don't stop with these pastels; there is no limit to the pale tints of colors. In fact, there is a pastel version of every color under the rainbow and then some.

Pastels work well in any room and with any decorating style, but these lighter tints are particularly perfect for those spaces where you want to escape and relax. These muted hues are subtle and light while still offering color to a space, and when combined with vibrant pops of color, they can add dramatic contrast and depth. By keeping things simple with pale walls, you can add interest with fun furnishings and bolder patterned accent pieces. Pair pastel hues with white or neutrals to open up your smaller spaces and reflect light. Representing freshness, femininity, peace, innocence, and simplicity, pastels have an adaptability that makes them a perfect choice for any space.

moll's thought

My husband has a lavender crewneck cashmere sweater that makes me giddy inside when he wears it. When I go shopping for baby clothes, the pale pinks, blues, and lavenders of those tiny little outfits make me feel warm and happy. Flowers like parrot tulips or lavender and pink roses speak to my senses! For me, pastels represent everything from sweet softness to super sexy.

SWEET COLORFUL DREAMS

Did you know that what you wear to bed can affect your whole evening and your night's sleep? Jump into bed in pastels and see how different you feel tonight and when you wake up in the morning! Softening pastels are soothing, and when I put on a pastel nightgown, I do feel softer and more relaxed. It's important to discover what colors represent to you—anything from a romantic evening to a satisfying good night's sleep.

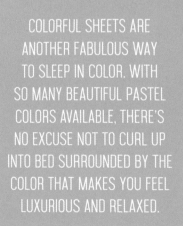

COLORFUL SHEETS ARE ANOTHER FABULOUS WAY TO SLEEP IN COLOR. WITH SO MANY BEAUTIFUL PASTEL COLORS AVAILABLE, THERE'S NO EXCUSE NOT TO CURL UP INTO BED SURROUNDED BY THE COLOR THAT MAKES YOU FEEL LUXURIOUS AND RELAXED.

WHAT YOU HAVE ON YOUR NIGHTSTAND IS ALSO IMPORTANT

Fresh flowers are a must-have. Find something with a scent that is soothing and refreshing to you.

Candles are great for ambiance. It's also handy to keep a lighter and flashlight nearby.

A book begging to be read and a journal and pen to write down your thoughts and goals are a great way to unwind. Have a well-placed lamp nearby, as well as eyeglasses, if needed.

Consider using a sound machine with a sleep coach to help you let go of the day, pray, and meditate.

Keep a photo of you and your loved one, or if you're single then a picture of you or a silhouette of two people that could represent a relationship that you want to bring into your life. Keep pictures of your kids out of the master bedroom.

Have a glass of water nearby, as well as anything else you need for comfort during the evening, so you don't have to leave your bed or room and interrupt your sleep.

Leave your electronics behind—no phones, computers, or iPads in bed.

FLOWER *power*

Cherry blossoms and other blooming branches offer a breath of fresh air and soften any space. Real cherry blossoms are available in early spring and mix beautifully with many other types of blossoms and branches such as dogwood, spirea, and even curly willow. When bringing branches into your home, make sure to cut the stems at an angle and hammer the ends a few times to allow them to soak up plenty of water. In a vase, tall bending branches balanced with shorter ones at the base and center create an easy, breezy, breathtaking arrangement.

#POP
OF COLOR

#SCOOTER

Who wouldn't want to scoot around and paint the town pastel? I admit that this feels more like a girl's ride, but don't you just want to jump on and go for a spin with flowers in your backpack, dressed in a matching ensemble? Although I wouldn't choose a pink car, I'd definitely pick a pastel pink scooter. The color we choose for our ride—even our bicycles—is a definite statement we want to make to the world and the people around us, even if we are totally unaware that's what we are doing.

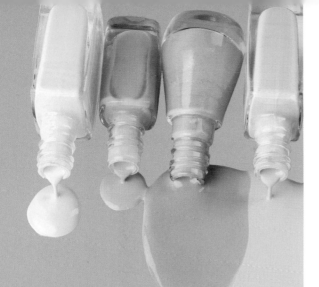

#NAIL POLISH

Nail polish colors and manicure trends are some of the most anticipated news for every fashion season. It's not just about the clothes the models are wearing, it's also about the hair, makeup, and nail color! Manicures seem to have originated in India with the use of henna as nail paint. China began using nail color as a way to indicate wealth and status, and soon the Egyptians followed the trend, making red polish popular. Nowadays, nail color trends change with the seasons, popularizing bright hues and pastels in the summer and deeper shades in the fall. Nail color lets you change your hue to fit your mood, whether you pump up the volume with bold colors or go soft and serene with pastels.

COLORFUL COCKTAIL

GRAPEFRUIT CAIPRIHINA

½ cup	fresh grapefruit juice
1	lime, juiced
2 ounce	Cachaca Rum
1 ounce	simple syrup (equal parts water and sugar boiled to a syrup) Crushed ice

Combine the grapefruit juice, lime juice, Cachaca rum, and simple syrup in a cocktail shaker with 2 ice cubes. Shake until chilled thoroughly, and pour over crushed ice. Garnish with a pastel petal or a soft flower like the one shown, plucked from a Dietes plant.

Consider working with a local artist who has created murals and can show samples of the finished work.

Look into art programs at your local university. There are many talented students looking for ways to offset school expenses and build their portfolios.

Stencils are easy to use. Also, there are art classes that teach different approaches to create simple designs that have a beautiful, elegant feel.

Wallpaper borders come in many designs and can be used around the perimeter of your space; then simply paint the ceiling or use faux techniques.

When faced with the dilemma of what to paint my master bathroom ceiling, I knew I needed to consult my dear friends and artists David Braly and Mark Montoya to come to the rescue with their incredible talent. Although I had a vision, I made the choice to share with them the pastel tones I wanted and then step back and let them do their thing!

TAKE PICTURES OF CEILINGS THAT INSPIRE YOU. MAGAZINES AND DESIGN BOOKS ARE GREAT SOURCES TO HELP YOU COMMUNICATE TO YOUR PROFESSIONAL EXACTLY WHAT YOU'RE VISUALIZING.

#COLORSTORY

I imagine everyone loves a garden or tea party. Who doesn't want an excuse to dress up and have some fun like we used to when we were kids? We would grab whatever we were allowed to play with from Mom's cabinet, mixing and matching dishes, cups, and saucers. It was marvelous! We'd sneak chairs from the house, and before we knew it, we had a lovely table set with Kool-Aid and PB&J sandwiches with the crusts cut off. There was no pressure, just pure joy and fun. Today, my garden parties include a tray of peach glassware, mint green chairs, and slightly more sophisticated sandwiches, but they're still an opportunity for childish delight.

Pastel colors became a huge trend in men's fashion during the 1980s. The show *Miami Vice* further popularized the pastel trend with soft shades showing up on shirts, suits, and filming locations.

Bianchi's signature bicycle color, Celeste, is a soft blue-green shade that the company is known to traditionally paint their bikes.

For the first time, the Pantone Color of the Year in 2016 was the blending of two pastel shades, Rose Quartz and Serenity. The color combo is a balance of warm and cool tones in soft, soothing shades, creating a sense of order, compassion, and peace.

The color Alice blue, a pastel tint of azure, was named after Theodore Roosevelt's daughter. She was married in a wedding dress that was a light shade of azure, which sparked quite a fashion trend, and the hit Broadway song "Alice Blue Gown" was inspired by her signature dress.

#SOFTENING PASTELS

> "EVEN A STRONG AND CONFIDENT WOMAN NEEDS TO ROCK A PASTEL EVERY NOW AND THEN TO STAY IN TOUCH WITH HER FEMININE SIDE.

— **MOLL ANDERSON**

REPEAT AFTER ME...
I CAN DO THIS
—unknown

#GROUNDING BLACK

Classic, sophisticated, seductive, and powerful, grounding black is a must-have for every space. Every woman needs a black dress in her wardrobe, and every room needs a touch of black. A timeless color, black anchors a space, creates structure and definition, and provides a dramatic backdrop to show off color. Black is the absence of light, but it is a powerful neutral that goes with any color palette, from the brightest hues to the softest pastels. There are many ways to add black to a room, such as with accessories and bold statement pieces. Black is also a classic choice to accentuate architectural details; this eye-catching color will make your details stand out—inside and out.

Black, the color of power, protection, and stability, has a contrast of meanings, from powerful and sophisticated to mysterious and evil. Black is said to absorb negative energy and offer protection from harm, and is a gateway to change, bringing the soul out of darkness and into the light.

moll's thought

When black became my signature color, I had absolutely no idea that the color black was the gateway to change. I believe it actually rescued me. It made me feel safe, protected me from negative energy, and enveloped me in a cocoon. Although I still love black and it will always be a statement color in my life, the difference today is that I also infuse vibrant color into my life and home, using black as a neutral.

CREATIVE FIX

This is what I would call a design moment, a happening that was effortless and took only a gut reaction to create. The gilded gold chair was one that had been in our home since 2007, after I bought it at a floor sale at Ralph Lauren. I knew immediately that this classic chair, which was upholstered with a fabulous, modern shiny black leather, would fit into any décor. That's a major characteristic of a smart purchase: a statement piece that will fit in any space and make a room come alive. While construction was underway and the framing of our walls was going up, it was easy to see where I would place our art. I envisioned it in this spot from that moment. It deserved a prominent place to be viewed; however, the problem was the frame on this piece was too earthy for the vibe I was showcasing. So I asked my faux artist Deb Staver to throw some silver leaf on it. A few hours later I tossed a beaded pillow on the chair, and *voila!*

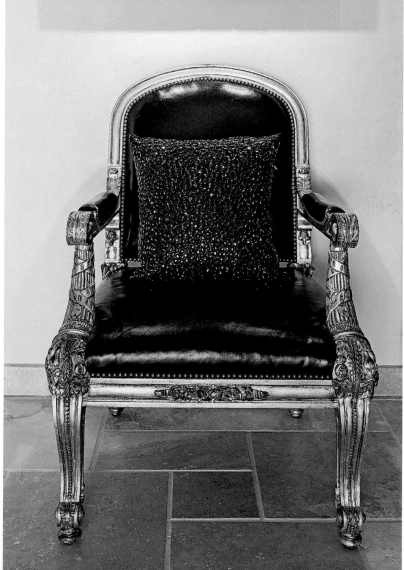

220

FLOWER *power*

#POP
OF COLOR

#AUTOMOBILE

An automobile is a major purchase for most, but did you know that the color you choose for your car says a lot about your personality? Think about the color of the car you own. If you own a black car, then you have chosen a car in the ultimate power color. The color black brings thoughts of black-tie dinners and chauffer-driven town cars or SUVs. Black is a classic, elegant color that makes us think of luxury. If you visualize owning a black car someday, you probably also dream of becoming financially successful. You may be longing for more depth in your life as well. Owning a black car means you not only want to be in control, but you plan to drive your way to the top.

Black calla lilies are sleek and elegant flowers. Even the name creates an air of mystery as they are not true lilies at all, and what appears to be a dramatic flower is actually a heart- or trumpet-shaped leaf. These striking stems are available year-round and stay fresh for up to 7 to 10 days. Several single stems in a vase are striking, or arrange them with other branches and blooms to create a more modern vibe. Calla comes from the Greek word for beautiful, and when speaking the language of flowers, calla lilies convey unique beauty and utmost respect.

#CLASSIC CARRY

There's nothing like a simple black purse in a beautiful leather to show you have great fashion sense and sophistication. Fortunately, looking chic doesn't have to cost a fortune and put you into debt. Get your inspiration from all the gorgeous "It Bags," and then invest in a "Classic Carry" that strikes your fancy and that's well made with the vibe that reminds you of your favorite designer bag. It was practicality that inspired a bag for women on the go around the turn of the twentieth century. Women wanted to be able to carry more than just a lipstick with them. As time went on, handbags became a major fashion and wealth statement, from Hermés with the "Kelly Bag," named after movie star-turned-princess Grace Kelly, to Coco Chanel's quilted-leather bag with a chain handle. Today, you don't have to be a celebrity to carry a fabulous "It Bag."

COLORFUL COCKTAIL

ROSEMARY BLACK & BLUE MARTINI

3	black olives
1 ounce	blue cheese
2 ounces	black vodka
1 ounce	sweet vermouth
1 ounce	black olive juice
1 tablespoon	fresh rosemary, plus 1 sprig for garnish

Stuff the black olives with the blue cheese. Place vodka, sweet vermouth, olive juice, and the rosemary in a cocktail shaker. Muddle the rosemary in the bottom of the shaker for 1 minute. Add 3 ice cubes to the cocktail shaker and shake until martini is well chilled. Strain into a martini glass and garnish with a rosemary sprig that has blue cheese black olives strung on it.

#COLOR
LESSON

The first stair rods were made of wrought iron—heavy but gorgeous. While owners of historic homes still love to use the iron, there are many choices of lightweight metal for your stair rods and finials that are easy to use.

Sisal is the number-one choice for my runners. If you want to go with a light color, make sure it's more of a speckled oatmeal tone since stairs are a high-traffic area. My go-to is a black wool sisal, which is so forgiving and looks great on any wood or stone stairway.

Leather borders along the edges of the runner give a bit of shine that's chic. There are wonderful vinyls that are thin and pliable that can give you the same look for less.

I love the look and luster that wood stairs provide, but safety for children and adults is always a concern. A black runner fastened directly to the stairs is a stunning way to get the best of both worlds!

STAIRWAYS ARE BOTH FUNCTIONAL AND A FABULOUS ARCHITECTURAL STATEMENT. YOUR RAILING IS THE PERFECT WAY TO SHOWCASE THE VIBE OF YOUR SPACE.

#COLORSTORY

Many people are thoughtful to hand down slightly used or worn furniture when they see a need. My mother once tried to give me a funky old gold chair. I turned it down because I didn't like it, only to have to sit on the floor with my son because we had no furniture. Not very smart! Looking back, I would have loaded up on the antique rug, funky chair, and old sofa that were in her garage. But after having to let go of furniture that I loved after my divorce, I was prideful and chose to go without, wanting to wait until I could get my feet on the ground before buying what I loved myself. Necessity forced me to dig deep, get real, and pray for creativity. Once I figured this out and got started, much to my surprise, I was pretty darn good at it. It's true that one person's discarded items are another person's treasure. If you're in need like I was, take a chance. Look at a piece like this big black sofa and ask yourself, "How can I make this work?" Even if a sofa has well-used cushions, you can cover them with a colorful throw and some fun pillows. It will make it super cozy and bring it back to life.

COLORFUL TRIVIA

Black was one of the first colors used in art, as artists worked with charcoal and made black pigments by burning bones and grinding natural elements into powders.

Black is the traditional color of taxicabs in England, and is the most common color for limousines and government officials' automobiles in America.

Black was not part of the wardrobe worn by nobles during the Middle Ages, with the exception of glossy, black sable, the most expensive and finest fur.

Black pepper is the most commonly traded and used spice around the world.

Made up of diamond, graphite, and amorphous carbon, Carbonado, known as the "black diamond," is the toughest form of natural diamond.

The black Givenchy dress worn by Audrey Hepburn in 1961 as Holly Golightly in *Breakfast at Tiffany's* is one of the most famous black dresses of the century.

#GROUNDING BLACK

> " I'LL STOP WEARING BLACK WHEN THEY INVENT A DARKER COLOUR.

WEDNESDAY ADDAMS

I AM STRONG, BECAUSE I'VE BEEN WEAK. I'M FEARLESS, BECAUSE I'VE BEEN AFRAID. I'M WISE, BECAUSE I'VE BEEN FOOLISH.

MADE BY
THEGOODVIBE.CO

CHANGE YOUR LIFE WITH
COLOR

YOU ARE THE COLOR
EXPERT

I'm so excited that you have made the decision to take emotional possession of your home and life. You're now on your way to understanding your "Color Story," and that's key to becoming your very own color expert. By beginning this unique and intimate look into your physiological feelings, childhood memories, and emotional responses to color, you will now understand what colors you're drawn to and why you love them so much, as well as what colors you've avoided and the reasons for your aversion to those hues. You have had this ability your entire life—this built-in "color perception."

I didn't realize until I started my journey to discover my color story that this perception is innate and available to all of us. Your sensory experiences allow you to become a colorist for you, as you become in tune with your senses. This will enable you not to be intimidated or out of your comfort zone when it comes to choosing colors for your home, your makeup, or your wardrobe. Choosing color for your home and family is choosing a more vibrant life that consists of energy, balance, and joy! You now have the confidence to live your life in living color.

What are you waiting for?

COMING TO YOUR SENSES

What color are you thinking of right now? Say it out loud and then write it down! There's a reason this color calls to you—it has the power to change your life. If more than one color comes to mind, maybe two or even three, then I want you to pay close attention because you may be putting your very first color combination together. I believe when you are drawn to more than one color at a time it's a harmonious match for you and a catalyst to the change you're hoping for. Yes, it can happen that fast. If you are already sensory aware, this process may move quickly since you are open to the discovery and excited to start your color rehab. As your senses awaken and come alive, you finally will have "come to your senses" and started creating a warm and inviting home.

ARE YOU READY FOR A CHANGE?

Ready or not, here comes the *wow* you've been waiting for! You are ready for this shift and you can make it happen starting this very minute! I've given you the tips, lessons, and stories to make this process easy, as you begin with simple, affordable changes. So let's not waste another minute—this weekend you could be holding a can of paint in a fabulous color and rolling away fear and doubt. You could be making colorful transformations into your home and life. I believe that once you do this, you will never regret bringing something as positive as color into your life, and when you see and feel the transformation it has on you, color will be your go-to for the rest of your life, your "Prescriptions of Color™" for change.

"TO FIND THAT **ONE** SPECIAL PERSON WHO WILL CHANGE YOUR LIFE, JUST TAKE A LOOK IN THE **MIRROR**
MOLL ANDERSON

WHAT'S YOUR COLOR STORY?

1. WHERE ARE YOU MOST DRAWN TO COLOR: IN NATURE, IN FOOD, IN FASHION, BEAUTY, ART, OR FURNITURE?

2. THINK OF A TIME RECENTLY WHEN YOU FOUND YOURSELF DRAWN TO A COLOR YOU NEVER THOUGHT YOU WOULD LIKE. WHAT WAS IT AND WHAT WERE THE CIRCUMSTANCES?

3. HAVE YOU EVER BEEN IN A RELATIONSHIP WITH SOMEONE OR MARRIED TO SOMEONE WHO LOVED A COLOR YOU HATED? DO YOU THINK YOU COULD LEARN TO LIVE WITH A COLOR COMPROMISE?

4. WHEN YOU BUY FLOWERS, DO YOU LIKE FLOWERS THAT ARE ALL THE SAME COLOR OR A MIX OF COLORS? IF ONE COLOR, WHAT COLOR? WHAT COLORS WOULD YOU MIX TOGETHER?

5. HOW DOES THE COLOR OF FOOD, AN OBJECT, OR PACKAGING INFLUENCE YOUR BUYING CHOICES? WOULD YOU EVER BUY ANYTHING IN A COLOR YOU DISLIKE?

6. WHAT NEW COLOR OR COLORS WOULD YOU LIKE TO INTRODUCE TO YOUR LIFE AND WHY?

7. WHAT COLOR BEST REPRESENTS THE CHANGE YOU WANT TO MAKE IN YOUR LIFE
   AND IN YOUR HOME?

8. HOW WOULD ADDING A NEW COLOR CHANGE THE MOOD OF YOUR SPACE?

9. IN WHAT WAY WOULD YOU INTRODUCE A NEW COLOR TO YOUR HOME? WITH PAINT,
   FURNITURE, OR ACCESSORIES?

10. WHAT IS THE COLOR OF HAPPINESS TO YOU?

TRY TO BE A RAINBOW
IN SOMEBODY ELSE'S CLOUD.

THE COLOR OF
GIVING

What is the Color of Giving?

Imagine the most beautiful rainbow made up of all the colors that fill your heart with joy. This is the color of giving. It's taking the "all about me" out of you.

The color of giving transports you to a place of living in the moment—a place where you can reflect upon what is happening in your community, your city, your country, and our world.

Many years ago, I heard a statement from Oprah that stuck with me: "Once you know better, you do better." This may seem like a small, commonsense idea, but when you discover the color of giving, even the simplest concept can grab hold of you.

The color of giving happens when we start thinking differently—it changes lives and we become alive in ways we never imagined. When we help others, we create meaning in our lives and reduce our stress levels by not focusing on our own problems.

It was not until I went on my first UNICEF trip to Jamaica that I understood the effects of limited access to clean water, which, according to the 2015 estimates of the WHO/UNICEF Joint Monitoring Program, affects a staggering 663 million people worldwide.[1] Although I've always done multiple things to conserve water, this trip affected me deeply and, contrary to my previously limited convictions about conservation, forever changed my view regarding the world's access to food and water.

Why was I so changed? What happened to move me so deeply?

Shortly after landing in Kingston, Jamaica, to take part in my first field visit with UNICEF, my husband, Charlie, called me to let me know that our beautiful home in Dallas was sitting in a foot of water. I was shocked, but my husband assured me that he would take care of things. Giving up control is not easy for me, but my commitment to UNICEF is so important to me. I was sitting in a van

with someone from UNICEF who has seen so much devastation and poverty, listening to her stories. There was no comparison; I would have to trust that Charlie could take care of things at home. In just a matter of hours, I would be witnessing programs for women and children who needed serious help. These were the real emergencies.

We traveled for hours up a winding, single-lane, makeshift road into the village of Maroon Town, cut off from electricity and water, and I thought to myself, "Wait a minute, no lights? No air-conditioning, no clean water, and makeshift roofs over their heads?" This was not the Jamaica I knew from the television commercials with the all-inclusive vacation packages, complete with spa, swimming pools, and exotic cocktails with colorful umbrellas! Those places are set on beautiful beaches. What I experienced was the real people of Jamaica and the real places where their families live.

However, we were immediately greeted by happy faces running toward us; children surrounded the vans, extending warm welcomes. I couldn't help but notice a huge, rusty bin. I asked one of the UNICEF representatives what the bin was for and the answer was shocking—it was there to capture water. The villagers would pray for rain to fill the bin with water; yet even if their prayers were answered and the bin was full, the

I am a passionate warrior for UNICEF and an advocate for women and children everywhere. I've just returned from my second field visit, this time with my husband, Charlie, to Mozambique, Africa. On this trip, we witnessed the service of programs that are each uniquely important. One instance that really touched my heart was when we visited a local hospital and UNICEF-supported health center where we met with mothers and children being screened for malnutrition. We saw year-old toddlers, who were smaller than our infant grandbabies, fighting for their lives; but we also got to see children who were recovered, chunky and happy due to this lifesaving program. When you see firsthand what a difference a program like this can make, it motivates you to want to do so much more. I was so thankful once again to witness UNICEF's lifesaving work.

As I physically remove my UNICEF armband, it is still emotionally embedded on my arm and in my heart forever!

villagers would still need water purification tablets provided by UNICEF to be able to drink the water.

But there is more. The villagers still have to get the water to their homes, and that is no easy task. They must fill a container with water and carry it over mountainous terrain in an area that is extremely unsafe, especially for the young girls who carry the water to their homes.

But what about those happy faces? The villagers were so happy to see us because we were wearing an armband or a t-shirt that signified UNICEF. When they see UNICEF, they see hope and, most importantly, they see help. Simply by putting on a UNICEF t-shirt I felt like I had suited up to be a defender of children—a defender of child rights, a defender of change and development, a defender who feels the call to help every day.

I am so proud to be a part of UNICEF. With offices in over 190 countries and territories, it promotes the rights and well-being of the world's children and has saved more children's lives than any other humanitarian organization. UNICEF tracks and reports on more than two hundred indicators that reveal the situation of children and women in the areas of education, health, gender equality, rights, and protection around the world.

UNICEF then uses collected information to design and implement programs to reach the most vulnerable children and families, from providing healthcare for prevention and treatment of diseases that contribute to the 16,000 preventable deaths of children each day worldwide, to identifying and educating the thousands of young girls, for whom learning can mean liberation from poverty, exploitation, and abuse. This data, along with our support, enables UNICEF to become the much-needed advocate for women and children globally.

But it doesn't stop there—entire communities are fostered by the assistance of UNICEF. By working in over one hundred countries to provide access to safe drinking water and adequate sanitation and educating people about the importance of hygiene, millions of people see the impact at scale, resulting in healthier, more sustainable communities. When they have access to sanitation facilities and clean water at school, girls are more likely to attend school along with boys, and the education provided continues to help the community advance.[2]

I consider my flooded home to be life-changing, in that it completely redirected my attention. Receiving that news while on this trip immediately forced me to recognize what was truly important. The needs of others were so obvious and abundant, and my flooded dwelling seemed insignificant in comparison. I was profoundly changed by my UNICEF visit to Jamaica, but even if you don't have the time or the money to travel across the world to help, there are many opportunities to make a difference right where you are; you often don't need to look much further than within your community and your circle of friends.

When we change our way of thinking, we come together and unite to help one another—creating a rainbow, the color of giving. Bringing our unique gifts and experiences, we contribute our true colors and form a beautiful rainbow with the power to color this world with kindness and love. We each play a part and have a distinct role, no matter how big or small, and it takes all of us, working together, to create

this magnificent rainbow. Even small and seemingly insignificant gifts make up the greater whole that changes the world. We all have the opportunity, but it starts with us exploring our own color stories and discovering our passions and what we are drawn to. When we get in touch with that, we'll realize ways we can contribute and spread joy in the color of giving.

We've all experienced the excitement and joy when we look up and see a rainbow in the sky. That's the color of giving you receive when you discover whatever it is you can do that makes a difference in one person's life or even the lives of an entire village.

Share the Color of Giving with Your Children

For more than 65 years, kids in the United States have helped provide medicine, proper nutrition, clean water, education and protection to other children around the world by participating in Trick-or-Treat for UNICEF. Help your children become superheroes for millions of children in need this Halloween. www.unicefusa.org/trick-or-treat

What can you do to shine the rainbow— the color of giving— to others?

Giving is represented in many different ways. Although we often think of money when we hear the word *give*, there is a multitude of ways to share the color of giving with those around you. And you'll discover that not only will you bring joy to others but you'll also reap benefits of that joy as well.

Research shows that people who give and are generous are typically more satisfied with their lives, regardless of their current situation. When they do encounter difficulties, they are generally better able to manage, possibly because they have an awareness that there are many others who are dealing with more difficult trials and situations.

Explore your strengths and use them to contribute to the rainbow of community. Even your struggles and lessons learned can help you to understand, relate to, encourage, and give hope to others. Find others who need that hope, and color their world.

Give of Yourself: Volunteer Your Time

I hear people say all the time, "Well, I can't afford to help," or "My five dollars won't make a difference." When I could not afford much financially, I gave what I could monetarily but also realized that my time is a valuable resource, and when it is all I can give, that is enough. Here are just a few ideas out of thousands to help get you started!

- Run an errand for an elderly person who is unable to get out easily, or offer to accompany them to a doctor's appointment.
- Deliver a care package to friends or family who are in the hospital. Include bottled water, a gift box of healthy snacks, or a book or favorite magazine.
- Offer to pet-sit, do laundry, or simply take in the mail for someone in the hospital, or their family member. These everyday things must still be done for someone whose loved one is in the hospital. What a blessing you could be.
- Help assemble care packages for missionaries or military overseas. Include a personal note letting them know you're thinking of them and appreciate their service.
- Reach out to a veteran or someone in the military who lives near you. Many returning home could use help readjusting to life. Wounded veterans may need rehab and physical therapy. Find ways to meet a need.
- Offer to walk or play with animals at a shelter. Donate food, old leashes, or dog beds. Better yet, adopt a furry new family member.
- Volunteer your time and skills in helping to build a house with Habitat for Humanity. (Visit their website for additional details: www. habitat.org)

Share Your Expertise: Mentor Others

Using your knowledge or skills to mentor others is truly a gift that can change lives in so many ways. Mentoring others, whether at work or in your community, is one way to pay it forward. As we reflect on our lives we can recognize and acknowledge those significant people who shared their knowledge and experience to guide us in our own journeys. Mentoring not only encourages and equips others, but in sharing our knowledge with others, we ourselves gain a feeling of value and confidence.

- Consider volunteering to tutor a child or teach adults to read. More than 10 percent of the world's population is illiterate.
- Teach someone basic computer skills to help equip them in finding employment.

Give Financially

Giving of your well-earned money, regardless of the amount, will truly bless others. No matter how much or how little you can give, there are so many worthwhile causes that can use the monetary help. And consider this: research has shown that when you spend your money to help others, it is much more satisfying and uplifting than when you spend it on yourself. The well-known adage is true: we feel so much better by what we give than what we receive.[3]

Don't Discard—Donate

I'm sure you've heard the saying, one man's trash is another man's treasure. Although you may have exhausted the use of your items, they can be valued necessities for others. Rather than discard your unwanted clothing, furniture, and household goods, donate them. There are many charities that can benefit from your used items.

- Goodwill not only uses the items in their stores, but the collection, sorting, and selling of donated items creates jobs for many people.
- The Salvation Army and many churches distribute donated items to people in need during natural disasters.

- Habitat for Humanity uses proceeds from the sale of donated items to build homes for those in need.
- Women's shelters are often in need of baby clothes, gently used baby items, and toys. Rather than toss or consign these items when your kids outgrow them, consider donating them to shelters that will give them to women and children in need.

Random Acts of Kindness

Coloring the world with kindness will make a lasting impact on others.

Those who happily give to others are generally healthier. When we are occupied with doing good for others, we are less likely to involve ourselves with negative emotions, which translates into a lower likelihood of depression and anxiety. By helping others, we create for ourselves a positive, healthy cycle: we feel better, which encourages us to participate in more acts of kindness.[4]

Share a Smile

The simplest gift you can give is a smile. Did you know that when you smile, the muscles in your face stimulate the brain, which releases endorphins that are responsible for making us feel happy? You may never know what a difference the simple act of smiling can have on others, but it's always heartwarming when you smile at someone and they smile back.

When you reach out and help others you reap the benefits as well.

UNICEF Kid Power is a revolutionary kids-helping-kids program® that gives kids the power to save lives. By getting involved with the UNICEF Kid Power Band, kids go on missions to learn about new cultures and earn points. These points unlock funding from partners, parents, and fans, and funds are used by UNICEF to deliver lifesaving packets of therapeutic food to severely malnourished children around the world. The more kids move, the more points they earn, the more lives they save.

EXTRA SPECIAL THANKS

My list of thanks continues to grow as I have been truly blessed with a wealth of friendships and an incredible and talented village of support who have mentored and believed in me over the years.

Always first, to my amazing husband and best friend, Charlie: Nothing happens without your support. You truly have the Midas touch, and I'm grateful and beyond blessed that you help and encourage me, even at a moment's notice—like pep talks at 3:00 a.m., hours of listening to my latest "aha" moment, watching *Super Soul Sundays* with me, and embracing and supporting all that I'm passionate about. Thank you for your beautiful, philanthropic heart. I love you more than words can express.

To all our children—Chase and Ashley Anderson, Mike and Aphrodite Camello, Hayley and Aaron Milam, and Lauren Anderson: You are all so very special and we are so proud of all of you.

To our five beautiful grandchildren—Gracie, Abby, Jacob, Scarlett, and Adrianna: I love you all so dearly and my life is richer because of my grandbabies.

To my beautiful mother, Mary Ellen Ruffalo: I love you to the moon and back. I promise to visit soon to sleep over at your place.

Bill Ruffalo, Courtney, Tiffany, and Molly: I always love you.

To my mother-in-law and father-in-law, Mama Hudda and Daddy Charles. I love you and thank you both for all your support.

To all my family, the Ruffalos, the Keaggys, the Becks, and the Andersons. Sis, Susan Anderson, I miss standing in my kitchen washing dishes together after the football games.

Karen Sue and John Hall—Time changes nothing between us. I love you both, and the drive to Dallas is do-able!

Brooke Burke-Charvet—I'm so grateful to have connected with you at this time in my life. You have been such a source of inspiration to me and I love you, BFF.

To Dr. Jim Sterling and Dr. Joey Hamilton, my brothers from another mother and the best diagnosticians in the world. Vester T. Hughes, I adore you.

Diane and Jim Rose—Thank you for the fun and for making the effort to be together.

To my L.A. girls, whose support goes above and beyond, Carolyn Conrad, Kim McKoy, Rebecca Meyer, Tomii Crump, Lisa Clark, Karine Joret, Brooke Anderson, Christina Binkley, Catherine Bach, Paulette Kam, and Dawn McCoy.

To Jan Miller Rich, my emotional twin and fellow dog-lover: I will not rest until I'm on your bestseller wall at Dupree Miller & Associates, between Tony Robbins and Joel Olsteen. Thank you for everything—and you too, Jeff Rich.

Lacy Lalene Lynch—you're the best; I love how you go after it.

To Sumya Ojakli at Simon & Shuster: Thank you for being my champion and getting it from day one.

To my lifetime girlfriends—Missy Anderson and Jinger Richardson: Thank you for the way you jump on planes to support me. I can't remember a time before y'all weren't in my life. Kitty Moon Emery, thank you for being my mentor and for being such an example of grace. Dee Haslam, I miss you and appreciate knowing that you're a phone call away. Bobbie

McCloud and Deb Staver, my Patton sisters and design partners for life. Nancy Lacy, we need a new snack now. Penny Brand, sister-friend, I love you. Cristina Ferrare, you are so freaking young and gorgeous! Paula Keane, we need to take it on the road, babe. Stacie Standifer Nichols, thanks again for *Nashville Lifestyles*. Linda Tarkington and the whole "Eden Rock vacation family, V-day!" Erica Reid, let's get together. Kimberly Chandler, always ready to say a prayer without notice. Sue Gragg, I love your amazing jeweled creations and the way you're my prayer warrior. Catherine Bloom, what would I do without you? Merri Lee Fox, for giving us style and beautiful things here in K-town. Sheryl Lowe, seriously miss you. Nancy Rogers, can't wait! Poteet and Terry Victory, I'm walking in high cotton with y'all!

I love my "Team Moll"—Cindy Games, Vice President and Publisher of Moll Anderson Productions, this is our fifth book, and we survived how many seasons of *The Bachelor* during this process? I will never forget that you gave me my first publishing deal. Thanks for believing in me still—and Winston and Harlow love you too. Ashley Cate, Creative Coordinator, wearer of many fab hats, daughter, assistant and calligrapher—honestly you are talented beyond your creative imagination and I know you are destined for something extra special in your life and career. Karen Hosack, how do you manage everything and throw my stuff on top of Charlie's? I'm so grateful! Sheri Swisher aka Ferguson, you have done all my books and since the last one you found your true love and married. Thanks for always hanging in there and doing such beautiful work. Linda Willey, Executive Director of the Charlie and Moll Anderson Family Foundation, you offer chicken soup, cocktails, laughs, and straight talk, four of my fave things. Loretta Cate, you will always be the "*Real* Housewife of Tennessee" and you're always 51 shades ahead of everyone. Suzanne Droese, PR, for helping me take on Texas. Pat-O, you are the rock and foundation of this house in Tennessee. Marilyn Spears, 11 years and counting! Elder Carillo, finally got your Gator—you're the best. Britta Bollinger, if I can dream it, you can do it with flowers. Peter and Rachel Van Ryder, Dallas has been quite the experience, over and over and possibly over again! Thank you for your management and loving my Winston and Harlow. Rachel, thank you for your creativity, flowers, and food.

To Brady Wardlaw, you have been there every step of the way! You have transformed me for the last 11 years—all 5 covers baby! I love ya! Chris Dylan, you are the best, soul brother and mad scientist with a brush. Christian Bier, you do glam style so fierce! Marylin Lee Spiegel, love your Zen you bring to me and your talent with your palette. Jeff Katz, you are such a true artist.

My UNICEF family, Caryl Stern, CFO—you inspire me daily and make me want to be a better person. How do you do all that you do and in so many countries? You are amazing and you do it all with sophistication, dignity, and grace. I'm honored to call you my friend. Chelsea Peters, the best travel companion to any foreign country hands down! Love your heart and how you break into song at a moment's notice. Jenn Lopez, how would we get Snowflake done without you? You're a wonder.

To the entire UNICEF organization, all over the world—for all you do every second of every day, thank you!

—Love, Moll

CREDITS

COVER

Nathan Schroder Photography—photography

Brady Wardlaw—hair and makeup artist

Thrush Holmes—art

Cygal Art Deco—table

CREDITS

DESIGN TEAM, *Knoxville, TN Residence*
Moll Anderson, Bill Algier,
Bobbie McCloud, Ron Hutchins,
Chris Joice

DesignWorks, *Bobbie McCloud*
1015 W Kirkland Avenue
Suite 306
Nashville, TN 37216
(615) 226-1081

Temptations, Inc.
Ron Hutchins, Chris Joice
Knoxville, TN

Bentwood of Dallas, *Bill Algier*
4508 Lovers Lane
Dallas, TX 75225
(214) 750-0271
www.bentwoodkitchens.com

Hickory Construction, *Mike Salley*
124 Kent Place
Alcoa, TN 37701
www.hickoryconstruction.com

SUBCONTRACTORS, *Knoxville Residence*
McGaha Electric
Edwards Plumbing
Mike's General Carpentry
Dennis Jessee, stone masonry
Joe Storm, tile subcontractor
Finish Point, interior trim sub
Rosebud, floor restoration
Auten Custom Hardwood Flooring
Custom Mirror and Glass

MNM Drywall
Garland Painting
Pizzolongo Plaster
Art-N-Stone, custom counter tops
Allen's Roofing
Elite Millwork
Preston Farabow, metal railings
R and G Iron Works, custom iron windows and doors
Go2Gals, *Becky Lee and Angie Davidson*

RESOURCES

ABC Carpet & Home
888 Broadway
New York, NY 10003
(212) 473-3000
www.abchome.com

Anichini—www.anichini.com

Arteriors—www.arteriorshome.com

Bennett Galleries & Co
5308 Kingston Pike
Knoxville, TN 37919
(865) 584-6791
www.bennettgalleries.com

Britta Bollinger—floral design
Knoxville, TN

Ceylon et Cie
Michelle Nussbaumer
1319 Dragon Street
Dallas, TX 75207
(214) 742-7632
www.ceylonetcie.com

Crate and Barrel
www.crateandbarrel.com

Cory Pope & Associates
1025 N Stemmons Fwy
Dallas, TX 75207
(214) 981-9119
www.corypope.com

David Sutherland
(214)742-6501
www.davidsutherlandshowroom.com

Deb Staver,
Faux finisher at Knoxville, TN residence
(615) 569-8072
Nashville, TN
deb.staver@gmail.com

Donghia—www.donghia.com

Fendi Casa—www.fendi.com

1stdibs, *Vintage pieces*
www.1stdibs.com

Forty Five Ten
4510 McKinney Ave
Dallas, TX 75205
(214) 559-4510
fortyfiveten.com

Frette—www.frette.com

G&G Interiors, *Merri Lee Fox*
5508 Kingston Pike
Knoxville, TN 37919
(865) 212-5639
www.gg-interiors.com

Glasshouse
919 Dragon Street
Dallas, TX 75207

Grange Hall, *florals*
4445 Travis St
Dallas, TX 75205
(214) 443-0600
www.ufgrangehall.com

Holloway's Custom Upholstery
4221 Ross Avenue
Dallas, TX 75204

Holly Hunt
1025 N Stemmons Fwy #590
Dallas, TX 75207
(214) 245-4770
www.hollyhunt.com

Javier Canamar,
Plaster work at Dallas, TX residence

John Salibello
New York, NY
www.johnsalibello.com

Laura Lee Clark
1515 Slocum St
Dallas, TX 75207
(214) 265-7272
www.lauraleeclark.com

Luna Smith
207 Dover Drive
Richardson, TX 75080
(972) 699-7823
www.lunasmithexpressions.com

Mansour Modern, *Benjamin Soleimani*
8606 Melrose Avenue
Los Angeles, CA 90069
(310) 652-9999
www.mansourmodern.com

Martin & Martin Design
1715 Market Center Blvd
Dallas, TX 75207
(214) 252-0692

Mecox
4532 Cole Ave
Dallas, TX 75205
(214) 580-3800
mecox.com

Ralph Lauren Home
www.ralphlaurenhome.com

Shine By S.H.O.
www.shinebysho.com

CREDITS

RESOURCES, *continued*

SubZero-Wolf, *Jim Bakke*
(kitchens, Dallas, TX and
Knoxville, TN residences)
www.subzero-wolf.com

Target—www.target.com

The Lamp Shoppe
1515 Dragon St
Dallas, TX 75207
(214) 741-5300
www.lampshoppedallas.com

Wired Custom Lighting, *Melineh Hacopians*
8607 Melrose Ave
West Hollywood, CA 90069
(310) 854-2800
www.wired-designs.com

Z Gallerie—www.zgallerie.com

PHOTOGRAPHY | CREDITS

A.K. Vogel—*page 100 (bottom right)*

Ashley Cate—*page 8 (top), 52(right), 56 (top), 67 (dinnerware), 81 (left), 84 (bottom), 123 (colorful cocktail), 153, 178 (flower power), 210, 225 (top)*

beall + thomas Photography—*page 84 (top), 237 (top)*

Eric Adkins Photography—*page 36, 38, 39, 50 (top), 58, 59, 72, 82, 148, 149, 177, 192, 193, 220, 221, 224*

Nathan Schroder Photography—*cover and pages 54, 55 (top), 64, 65, 68, 69 (middle, bottom), 73, 79, 86, 87, 93, 94, 95, 98, 101, 106, 107, 110, 114, 115, 121, 124, 125, 129, 135, 138, 139, 140, 142, 152, 154, 157, 163, 180, 182, 183, 186, 187, 198, 201, 228, 229*

Jeff Katz Photography—*pages 10, 255*

Kristen Brady—*pages 8 (bottom), 9*

Leigh Ann Chatagnier—*colorful cocktails, pages 67, 81, 97, 109, 165, 179, 195, 209, 223*

Michael Gomez Photography—*pages 17, 53 (colorful cocktail), 92, 151 (colorful cocktail), 206, 237 (bottom)*

Simon Glenn Michael, Inc.—*page 70*

@mollanderson Instagram—*48, 61, 62, 75 76, 89, 90, 103, 104, 117, 118, 131, 132, 145, 146, 159, 160, 173, 174, 189, 190, 203, 204, 217, 218, 231, 242, 243*

ART

Thrush Holmes, Bill Lowe Gallery—
cover and pages 154, 228, 229

David Braly—*pages 56–57 (ceiling),
210 (ceiling)*

Brian Rutenberg, Forum Gallery—
pages 64, 148, 149

Christopher Martin, Christopher Martin
Gallery—*pages 73, 98, 115, 124*

Hyunmee Lee, Bill Lowe Gallery—
pages 79, 84

George Condo—*pages 82, 142, 163*

Allen Cox, Bennett Galleries & Co—*page 84*

Harold Krauss, G&G Interiors—*page 87*

Michael David, Bill Lowe Gallery—
pages 106, 107, 112

Poteet Victory, McLarry Modern—*page 121*

Kevin Archer, Bill Lowe Gallery—*page 129*

Tommie Rush, Bennett Galleries & Co—
page 129 (glass sculpture)

Richard Heinsohn, Bill Lowe Gallery—
page 135

Dirk De Bruycker—*page 140*

Hanson Gallery, Knoxville—*pages 148, 149
(glass art)*

Alfredo Bovio Di Giovanni, Bill Lowe
Gallery—*page 192*

Malcolm Rains, Meyer Gallery—*pages 193*

Braldt Bralds, Gerald Peters Gallery—
page 220

Sam Glankoff, Bill Lowe Gallery—*page 221*

Richard Currier, Bill Lowe Gallery—*page 224*

Daniel Motz, Bill Lowe Gallery—*page 224*

NOTES

1. www.unicef.org/statistics

2. www.unicef.org

3. https://positivepsychologyprogram.com/
spending-money-can-promotes-happiness

4. http://yakezie.com/198573/lifestyle/
the-benefits-of-giving-to-others

MOLL ANDERSON

Moll Anderson is an accomplished author, television and radio host, interior designer, life stylist, and global advocate for women and children. Moll's career has been filled with many professional achievements, including winning an Emmy for her work as an entertainment reporter; being chosen as one of Donna Karan's Women Who Inspire; and as a three-time recipient of the Gracie Awards, which recognize outstanding programming created by women and about women, as well as individuals who make exemplary contributions to the industry.

Moll is a woman of many trades. Her lifestyle and interior design acumen have been enthusiastically embraced by readers of her four home and lifestyle books. She has been a regular contributor to *The Doctors* television show and a guest co-host on *FABLife*, and she has appeared on numerous other television shows, including *Access Hollywood Live*, *Good Day LA*, *The Talk*, *Good Morning America*, *The Today Show*, and *Dr. Phil*. Moll has been featured in national publications such as *InStyle*, *Cosmopolitan*, *USA Today*, *Huffington Post's Women in Business*, as well as in regional publications.

Along with her professional work, Moll is a dedicated philanthropist, focusing her energy on many deserving causes. She commits her time and resources to improving the lives of women and children in her community and internationally through her work with such organizations as Habitat for Humanity and UNICEF. Moll received the Spirit of Compassion Award at the 2016 UNICEF Snowflake Ball.

For more information visit MollAnderson.com. Moll can also be followed on Twitter (@mollanderson), Instagram(@mollanderson), Facebook (facebook.com/mollanderson), Pinterest (pinterest.com/mollanderson), and YouTube (youtube.com).

IF YOU KNEW YOU COULD CHANGE YOUR LIFE IN ONE WEEKEND AND CLEAR OUT THE COBWEBS OF YOUR PAST WITH COLOR AND A BRUSH, WOULD YOU DO IT?

———

MOLL ANDERSON